Rice Coo

Neera Verma

DIAMOND BOOKS

ISBN : 81-7182-541-9

© **Author**

Publisher
DIAMOND POCKET BOOKS (P) LTD.
X-30, Okhla Industrial Area, Phase-II
New Delhi-110020
Phone : 011-51611861-865
Fax : 011-51611866
E-mail : sales@diamondpublication.com
Website : www.diamondpublication.com

Edition : 2004

Price : Rs. 100/-

Concept and Design of Cover and Text :
Media Plus, Delhi-110092

Printed at
Adarsh Printers,
Navin Shahdara, Delhi-110032

Contents

About This Book

Everybody likes palatable and delicious food and, for any food to be tasty, it is not necessary to spend money and energy. You can yourself feel satisfied and earn approbation from others by serving the food that satiates taste buds.

It has been well said that if you wish to win a person's heart, the easiet way is to reach his heart through his tongue.

Food is an inseparably essential part of our life. No doubt, food is the demand of our body, but a tasteless and unsuitable food neither nourishes body nor does it meet our requirements of tongue and taste as one can relish one's food only when it is tasty, having all the requisite ingredients.

In this book many unique and delicacies rice-based distinct have been detailed, in an understandable way, not only for the benefit of adept housewives but also for the novice ladies who are not much adept in the art of preparing variable food preparations.

Cooking: An Art

Cooking an art, in itself, which can win any person's heart and favour. Everybody has weakness for delicious and tasty food, as it is simply due to liking or weakness for a particular type of food delicacy that new restaurants, eating houses, food jaunts are coming up almost everyday and each food outlet specialises in one food delicacy or the other. We always rush to the food outlet where our taste buds can be satiated and our urge for a particular type of food is met with.

Appetite is the first and foremost urge or feeling of a new-born child, as each child satiates his need for feeding through milk only. The joy and satisfaction a person derives after taking his food, is beyond description. Satisfaction and satiation are the two measurin rods of a good food. Whatever food we take must meet our body requirements. But, if such a food is prepared in an artistic way, and is served with a smiling face, it adds to its taste. Good food is a source of joy for the person who serves and also to whom it is served. But for a food to be useful, it must be useful, nutritious and tasty.

Good food served in any marriage party, is remembered by all the invitees and people can ill afford to forget that of having been served a tasty, delicious, delectable food. People accord more significance to food which has comeliness and grace of the couple. Food is an essential part of our deit daily life. No doubt food is an irresistible need of our body but any food gulped down the gulleto reluctantly can adversely affect our health and food taken with full indulgence and interest is a boon to our body, provided it is tasty, nutritious and inclusive of all the essential ingredients.

How to Prepare Delicious Food

Man is a social animal and it is an old custom to visit someone at his house and invite others to your place. This is an unending course of exchange of visits. Respecting and receiving a guest is a part of our culture. If you visit someone, it is customary to serve some eatables which is a sign of love and affection. If the food items served are not tasty entire affection is relegated to the hind seat. But if the food items served are tasty and delicious, you will nurture nature the sweet memories about the good food served to you. In return, when you visit a guest, you will also take alongwith you some sweet remembrances of the delicious food served to you.

To serve and be served is a matter of habit with some people. Taste is the basic ingredient of all living beings. Each person tries to carve out variable delicacies out of the food (raw food) items available and, no doubt, it is a way to earn popularity, apart from enjoying your food. Exchange of food patterns is fast growing all over the globe. Western Countries politically hesitate to make friends with the chinese but have no reservation and hesitation in acquring and consuming chinese food. Even to Indians chinese food is popular, right from corner food jaunts to 5-star hotels.

An adept housewife nurtures a burning desire to cook food of such a high quality that all persons pay tributes to her for her cooking keeping this desire in view we wish to make you a perfect houswife and a successful cook to enable you to prepare delicious food items, by following the instructions and guidelines penned down in this book. Hence, various easy-to-do and popular cooking devices and methods have been suggested in this cook, for the benefit and use of all the housewives.

Artistic Presentation of delicacies

It is true that preparing tasty and delicious food is an art of high order. But all your efforts will fail if your method of serving and presenting the food items is erratic or you are not well conversant in this art. Hence, it is necessary that you should not only be perfect in preparing good food but also equally adept in serving and presenting the same.

In order to succeed in booth the said modes, it is not essential to have additional apparatus, rather the apparatus, at hand, will suffice to meet the requisite requirement. First of all, you have to keep your dining table neat and clean. In addition the dining table, plates, saucers, forks, spoons, glasses, pieces of cloth and tissue paper should be placed well on the dining table itself. So much so for decoration of the dining table. But more important factor is as how and in what way you serve your delicious food to your guests. For instance, if you heap up (in case you are serving salad) radish, beet, green chillies, green corriander (leaves), tomato in disordered fashion on a large plate it will give a bad look. If all the said ingredients are thoroughly sliced, cut and spread in a plate in a tasteful and artistic way, it will earn appreciation of your guests.

It will add a grace to your food if the same is served with a cheerful mood and artistic bent it will certainly add grace to your food and presentation. These rules should be followed at each and every time as a matter of habit and not when some guests are to feted and served with food. This way not only your food, service and presentation will earn you kudos from your guests but it will become a trait of your personality and taste.

Upkeep of Kitchen

For upkeep and beauty of kitchen, many ultra modern

implements are available in the market which not only render your food tastier but also help to save fuel. First of all we should see what type of kitchen we have and also whether all the necessary requirements are available in the kitchen. Is there proper arrangement for light, water and air? Do we actually pay attention to cleanliness and hygiene also?

As cleanliness (rather purity) of mind and body is a pre-requisite for an ideal health, so is the requisite cleanliness of kitchen imperative for processing good food. Hence cleanliness and neatness in kitchen are the primary pre-requisites of a good kitchen.

If possible, keep your kitchen well equipped will all the modern equipment/apparatus. Let us discuss the equipment with whose help we can prepare food, without tiring ourselves. Cooker, toaster, tandoor, are available in the market. These implements and goods help us in preparing food. All eatables, like raw and cooked vegetables etc. should be stored in a frige to avoid wastage.

Bind an apron around your waist and then enter your kitchen. It will prevent your clothes being soiled by dirty hands or when condiments have been handled. It will also not let drop oil lets fall on your clothes. It is convenient to cook food while standing and for there should be cemented shelf. Keep all the requisite articles and implements nearby you so that you do not have to run hetter and sketter to find out the needed object. Do not spread vegetable skin peelings while slicing nor spread water here and there at the floor.

You should remember that kitchen is reflective mirror of your personality. In fact tasteful upkeep, cleanliness can motivate and energise you to prepare food in an artistic way.

The art of serving food
The next important aspect is the art of serving food. If meals

are to be served in a traditional way while sitting, clean the floor, place a wooden plank/patra and spread white sheet thereon. Then serve food in Thalis (steel plates), though dining table culture is rampantly in vogue these days. Do not talk while taking your meals and if that be absolutely necessary, then try to use minimum word. Do not serve all the food items in one go, rather serve as and when demanded and needed, and also do not force or insist anybody to eat more.

No doubt there are plenty of books available in the market on the art of cooking, but a book that imparts and guides the housewives, about complete information is hardly available and absence of such a type of book is a dire necessity of the hour. These books will ably fill-in the gap. Not only that but any housewife can earn Kudos and approbation from her guests, if she can practise the novel methods suggested for cooking and preparing tasteful and mouth watering food items.

Hopefully, this book will help you to specialise in the art of cooking food and then you will be able to fascinate your guests and acquaintances by serving them tasty meals. You can adjust quantity and measurements of oil, material, condements etc. according to your, taste choice and requirements, though every possible care and caution has been taken in detailing about such ingredients and facts. All said and done, the author, publisher and the printer cannot be held liable in case any printing mistake has inadvertantly crept in, despite best efforts and intentions.

—NEERA VERMA
K-45, Jangpura Extension,
New Delhi — 110 014

I. EVERGREEN FOOD PREPARATIONS

MASALA RICE

INGREDIENTS

200 gms Rice	3 small sized potatoes
1 TSP — cumin	3 small sized bringals
½ cup oil	½ TSP Garam Masala
Table salt — according to taste	3 small green onions (without green leaves)
Green leaves of Corriainder	½ TSP Red Chillies
½ Cup green peas boiled	½ Cup grated coconut
	½ TSP sugar (crystol)

METHOD OF PREPARATION

Finely grind corriander, Red Chillies, Cumin sugar, Garam Masala, Coconut etc. to paste form, but sprinkle some water over these ingredients before grinding.

Cut each potato into 4 pieces. Cut bringals also into 4 pieces each but take care they do not get segregated (Separated)

Heaten oil in a stewpan (karahi) and fry masala laden vegetables. Thereafter add some water and then cover the pan.

Cook rice in double the quantity of water (400 ml) and then add already fried vegetables and cover and heaten on slow fire. When water contents evaporates, remove the same from fire.

VEGETABLE PULLAO

INGREDIENTS

3 cups Rice

100 gms green peas

1 TSP cumin (Roasted)

8 cloves

salt — to taste

800 gms sliced cauliflower

1/4 cup Raisins

3 sliced onions

1 TSP black pepper

1 Pc. Ginger (Shiced)

3 sliced carrots

1 cup curd/yogart (Fresh)

6 TBSP Ghee.

4 Bay leaves (Tej Patta)
 / cassia leaves

100 gms Hya cinth
 beans (sliced)

2 cardamom

1 Pc. Cinnamon (dalchini)

METHOD OF PREPARATION

Heaten ghee in a pan and add onions, cumin, cloves, cardamom, cinnamon, black pepper and ginger, and fry till it is brown.

Now add the vegetables to the above contents and fry for 2-3 minutes. Then add curd to it.

Fry rice in ghee, add 3 cups of water and cook, but keep on slow fire.

When rice is fully cooked, add vegetables and add some water and a TSP of ghee also.

If the Pullao is prepared in a cooker the same will be ready after 2 whistles.

TOMATO RICE (PULLAO)

INGREDIENTS

> 2 cups Rice
> 1 cup tomato juice (Fresh)
> 1/2 cup mustard (seeds)
> 4 TBSP ghee
> 1/2 TSP cumin
> 4 cloves
> salt, to taste
> 3 cups water
> 5 Black pepper
> 1 Pc cinnamon
> 3 green chillies
> 1/2 TSP Turmeric Powder

METHOD OF PREPARATION

Heaten ghee and fry rice in it, then add boiled water and tomato juice. Cover the utensil and let the contents cook on slow fire.

Heaten ghee in a frying pan. Add green chillies, black pepper, Cumin, cloves, cardamom to it and fry. Then add salt and turmeric and let it cook.

Remove from fire after water content has evaporated. Now relish tomato Pullao.

RICE PARANTHAS

INGREDIENTS

    150 gms Rice flour

    50 gms Besan (flour of grams)

    25 gm onions

    1/2 TSP Garam Masala

    Salt to taste

    Corriander leaves (fresh) chopped

    1 TSP chopped ginger,

    2 green chillies

    1/4 TSP turmeric (powder)

    ghee (for frying)

METHOD OF PREPARATION

Mix rice powder with flour of Besan and wheat. Add some quantity of ghee and all chopped / pounded condiments. Knead all the contents, after adding curd.

Work out a thick paste and roll. Now fry on fire. Be careful while turning upside down and vice versa as the paranthas can crack.

RICE PAKAURAS

INGREDIENTS

250 gms gram flour/Besan
1 TSP corriander (pounded)
2 green chillis,
Chopped green corrinder
1 pinch of asafoetida (Heeng)
1 pinch of sodium bi carbonate
1 Pc (whole) ginger
1/2 TSP Red chillies
1 TSP Garam Masala
Salt to taste
Ghee

METHOD OF PREPARATION

Let the rice remain soaked in water overnight. In the morning drain out water and then let it dry in the sun. After it dries, pound it well and prepare a fine paste on a pastel. Sift/filler in a sieve.

Add a pinch of soda bicarbonate and other ingredients spices. Also add ginger, green chillies, chopped corriander leaves.

Shuffle the contents, adding some water quite often. Heaten ghee in a stewpan and, when ghee turns quite hot, taper the flame. Now process small sized Pakauras out of the paste prepared previously. Now fry the Pakauras in the ghee. Pakauras will turn bigger in size as soon they are put in ghee.

When Pakauras assume brown colour, serve hot.

PLAIN RICE (SALTISH)

INGREDIENTS

250 gms Rice
1 ladle (karhchhi) ghee
500 gms water
Salt

METHOD OF PREPARATION

Pour water in a pan, mix salt and rice for being put in water. Heaten on slow fire. When entire quantity of water dries, remove the pan, but let it remain covered. When rice gets fully cooked, put in ghee. Now delicious rice dish is ready for being served with cooked pulse.

PLAIN RICE

INGREDIENTS

250 gms Rice
500 gms water

PROCESS

Wash rice, after divesting the same of dirt and other elements. Put rice in water and place on fire. Rice will soften after 1-2 lodings. Remove the gruel. Now rice are ready for being served.

Plain rice are better relished when taken with cooked kidney bean (green moong dal).

ONION PULLAO

INGREDIENTS

    250 gms Rice
    2 Pcs (whole) onion
    1/2 TSP Garam Masala
    Salt to taste
    500 gms water
    1/2 TSP Cumin
    1 TSP Ghee

PROCESS OF PREPARATION

Clean the rice and soak in water.

Reduce one onion to small pieces, after peeling the outer skin and fry in 1/2 TSP of ghee. Roast Cumin in residual 1/2 TSP of ghee. Now remove rice from water and fry in ghee (1/2 TSP). Put in sliced pieces of onion, salt and garam masala shuffle the contents 2-4 times and let it cook on (slow) fire.

When rice are fully cooked, sprinkle fried/roasted onion pieces and serve.

COCONUT PULLAO

INGREDIENTS

    1 Pc. Fresh coconut (Raw)

    1 TSP cumin

    1 Pc lemon

    1 TSP cooking oil or ghee

    200 gms Rice

    1 TSP green/fresh corriander (chopped)

PROCESS

Soak the rice in water after cleaning, heaten oil/ghee in a pan and put in cumin also and fry rice in it.

Grate coconut and retain its water. New mix coconut water, green corriander, salt and lemon juice. Put the same in requisite quantity of water and cook. After the preparation has fully cooked, spread coconut (grated) contents over it and serve.

Cheese Pullao

INGREDIENTS

 200 gms Rice

 1 TSP Cumin

 Green Corriander leaves

 Salt to taste

 250 gms cheese

 Green chillies

 2 TSP oil or ghee

 1/2 TSP Garam Masala

PROCESS

Clean rice and soak in water.

Slice cheese into small cubes (200 gms) and rest of the quantity (50 gms) should be grated. Heaten oil/ghee and fry cheese cubes and put in 400 gms water to cheese cubes. Fry cumin in the same oil/ghee, then pour in juice in the same and fry slightly. Put in water and cheese therein. Put in also garam masala and salt, and let the contents cook.

ZARDA PULLAO

INGREDIENTS

    200 gms Rice

    50 gms pure Desi Ghee (clarified butter)

    100 gms crystal sugar

    Saffron flakes

    100 gms (hot) milk. (cow's milk)

    100 gms assorted dry fruits

    1 Pc lemon

PROCESS

After cleaning rice, let it soak in water for two hours.

Dissolve saffron and sugar in milk and season the liquid with desi ghee.

Boil rice in a separate pan. Pick up one rice grain and when the same has fully cooked, mix seasoned liquid with it and then cook properly.

Thereafter mix lemon juice and shuffle properly so that lemon juice gets suitably mixed with rice. Finally, mix dry fruits and enjoy delicious taste of zarda (saffron) Pullao.

Mushroom Rice

INGREDIENTS

200 gms Rice
2 Pcs Tomato
50 gms cheese
1 TBSP Pure Desi ghee
200 gms mushroom (Fresh)
2 Pcs onions
1/2 TSP black pepper
1 TBSP cooking oil
Salt to taste

PROCESS

After cleaning rice, let it soak in water for half-an-hour, reduce mushroom to small pieces and then fry in vegetable oil.

Also fry chopped pieces of onion and tomato and mix black pepper also, for being fried in balance quantity of oil. Mix the previously fried ingredients with it (that is finally chopped pieces of mushroom and grated cheese and let all the contents cook for 4-5 minuts on slow fire.

Heaten pure ghee and mix (soaked) rice with it and let it be fried in pure desi ghee. Now add salt to taste, put in some water and let it cook. Finally garnish the rice top with mushroom (already fried) before you serve to your guests.

MADRASI PULLAO

INGREDIENTS

- 250 gms Rice (Fully cleaned)
- 1/2 TSP Mustard seeds
- 1-1/2 TSP Red Chillies
- curry leaves
- 500 gms urad ki dal (Horsebean)
- 1/2 TSP Til (Gingelly)
- 11/4 TSP Salt
- 2 TSP Ghee

PROCESS

Clean rice and boil and let it cool. Then mix salt and til to it.

Pour ghee in a pan and fry horsebean, also adding mustard seeds and curry leaves to it. Now fry rice in the aforesaid ingredients. After the first boil, your Madrasi Rice is ready.

SWEETENED PULLAO

INGREDIENTS

250 gms Rice

1/2 litre milk

4 Nos. Cardamom

4 Nos. Bay leaves (Tej Patta)

100 gms Ghee

150 gms sugar

8 Nos cloves

1 Pc Cinnamon

Saffron (a few flakes)

100 gms assorted dry fruits

PROCESS

Let the rice remain soaked in water for half-an-hour

Heaten ghee in a pan and mix cloves, bay leaves and cinnamon to it. Mix the ingredients throughly and add rice. After frying the rice and other contents for sometime, remove the same from fire.

Pour water in another pan (750 gms) and boil till it is reduced to a syrup form. Mix saffron with the syrup.

Mix syrup with rice and add milk to the contents and let the mixed ingredients be cooked. When rice is half cooked, reduce the flame. When fully cooked, garnish with dry fruits.

KHICHRI

INGREDIENTS

250 gms Rice
1/2 TSP cumin
1/2 TSP turmeric powder
A pinch of asafoetida (heeng)
150 gms kidney Bean (Moong ki dal)
1/2 TSP Red chillies
Salt to taste
Ghee

PROCESS

Wash dal and Rice properly.

First fry it afoetida in ghee and then fry in cumin seeds in the same ghee. Finally add turmeric and red chillies (powder) to it. Mix the ingredients with the help of a large spoon and then add Rice and kidney bean to it. After frying the same for 3-4 minutes, add 3 glassful of water, add salt and let the contents cook.

Serve after the contents have been fully cooked.

SALTISH MILK PULLAO

INGREDIENTS

Rice 250 gms
1 Pc ginger (whole)
1 bundle green mint leaves
1/2 TSP salt
10 gms almonds
10 gms pistaschio
50 gms cream
Saffron flakes
1 bundle green corriander leaves
100 gms onions
1/2 TSP corriander seeds
100 gms Raisins
4 TSP Ghee

PROCESS

Properly wash rice in water. Grind ginger, green corriander and mint leaves to fine paste form and fry the contents in ½ quantity of ghee. Cut each onion into 2 pieces each and then boil. After onions have been boiled, remove the onion pieces from water and add rice to the resultant liquid. When rice is on the verge of softening (during the boiling process) add mixture (paste) of above ingredients. After sometime remove from fire. Add salt and powdered corriander to it and mix thoroughly.

Mix saffron with cream and then add to cooked rice. Finally mix the dry fruits to processed rice.

POTATO PULLAO (ALU PULLAO)

INGREDIENTS

200 gms Rice

1 TSP salt

4 Nos cloves

1 Pc cinnamon

50 gms ghee

100 gms Potatoes

1 TSP red chillies

4 Nos cardamom

2 Nos Bay leaves

PROCESS

Soak rice in water. Slice potatoes into small pieces and lightly fry.

Heaten ghee and fry cloves, cardamom seeds, bay leaves and cinnamon in it. All the ingredients should be added to rice. Add requisite quantity of water. Add fried potato pieces, salt and red chillies also. Remove from fire when ready.

KESARIYA PULLAO

INGREDIENTS

     200 gms Rice
     100 gms Ghee
     Small quantity of saffron flakes
     10 gms Raisins
     3 Nos cloves
     200 gms sugar
     2 Nos Cardamom
     50 gms coconut (dry)
     10 gms chironjia (sapida)

PROCESS

Let the rice remain soaked in water for an hour. Heaten ghee in a pan and roast cloves in the ghee. Remove water from rice and season the same, until it turns brownish/rosy. Now add a glassfull of water to the contents and let it cook.

When water has evaporated mix saffron with milk, adding sugar to it, mix with rice. Remove from fire and add (pulverised) cardamon, raisins and grated coconut. Now your kesaria pullao is ready for being served.

BESANI PULLAO

INGREDIENTS

200 gms rice
100 gms oil
1/2 TSP turmeric (powder)
Green corriander leaves
200 gms besan (flour of gram pulse)
1 TSP red chillies powder
1/2 TSP garam Masala
1 TSP cumin
Salt to taste

PROCESS

Mix Besan, salt and red chillies (powder) and process rolls. Boil the same in water. Slice the boiled rolls into small pieces (popularly known as Gattas).

Add requisite quantity of water of rice and place on fire in a pan. Fry cumin in ghee, and mix the same with rice, along with besan cubes. Mix salt, red chillies, turmeric and garam masala and mix all the ingredients. When rice soften, remove from fire and add chopped corriander leaves or garnish the preparation with corriander leaves.

Arhar Pullao (Pigeon Pea Pullao)

INGREDIENTS

    125 gms Rice

    2 Pcs onion

    2 TSP ghee or oil

    1/4 TSP turmeric (powder)

    1 Pinch asafoetida

    125 gms Pigeon Pea

    2 Pcs Tomato

    1/2 TSP red chillies (powder)

    2 Nos green chillies

    Salt to taste

PROCESS

Properly clean Rice and Pigeon pea/pulse and let both remain soaked in water for 2 hours.

Put oil or ghee in a pan and fry chopped onion, green chillies and asafoetida.

Mix red chillies, turmeric and salt in half cupful of water and fry the same, also adding fried onion pieces to the same. When the ingredients have been fully fried; add finely chopped tomato pieces to it. When all the ingredients have been fully fried, add rice and pigeon pea (pulse) to same. Put in 350 gms of water and let it cook for two minutes, after which remove the contents from fire.

SOYABEAN PULLAO

INGREDIENTS

1 Cup soyabean Bari (dried small pounded lump of soybean)
1 Pc onion
Green corriander leaves
1 TSP pulverised Dhania (Corriander seeds powder)
3 TSP oil
2 Cups Rice
2 Pcs tomatoes
1/2 TSP turmeric powder
1/2 TSP garam masala
1 TSP salt

PROCESS

Soak soyabean Baris in water which should be fried in oil till they assume large size. Clean rice and soak in water.

All the spices should be pounded and reduced to paste form. Slice onion into small pieces. Now fry all the ingredients along with onion and fry until it turns golden. Add soyabean baris and then add rice also. After frying the contents for some time, add 4 cups of water and cover with lid and place on fire. When rice cook fully, remove from fire. Lastly, spread chopped corriander leaves over cooked rice.

Mewa Pullao

INGREDIENTS

100 gms Rice (Basmati variety)
1 TSP Garam Masala
2 TSP Pure Desi Ghee
Green corriender leaves
200 gms assorted dry fruits
1/2 TSP Red chillies
Salt to taste

PROCESS

Soak Rice for 2 hours in water. Thereafter heaten ghee and fry rice. When fried, add red chillies and salt to which 400 gm water should be added, and let the same cook.

Separately roast dry fruits in a stewpan, when rice has boiled partly (not fully boiled) mix all the dry fruits, cover with a lid and put off fire. Let the contents cook in the steam and heat generated in the pan.

After 5 minutes, add garam masala and spread/garnish green corriander at the top.

CHANA PULLAO

INGREDIENTS

 2 cups basmati rice
 2 Pcs onions
 1 Pc ginger
 Green corriander leaves
 1/2 TSP red chillies
 2 TSP veg. Oil
 1 cup — boiled and soaked black gram
 4 cloves of garlic
 Salt, to taste
 1 TSP Garam Masala
 1/2 TSP Turmeric powder

PROCESS

Wash rice and soak in water.

Chop onion and garlic into small pieces and fry in ghee. Fry boiled black grams. Now add salt, red chillies, turmeric and garam masala to it.

Pour 4 cups of water in a pan and cook rice. Mix thoroughly roasted black grams and cooked rice and remove from fire. Now spread corriander leaves (finely chopped) over it.

ELEPHANT'S FOOT PULLAO (ZIMIKAND'S PULLAO)

INGREDIENTS

    2 cups rice
    3-4 cloves of garlic
    4 Nos. green chillies
    11/2 TSP Turmeric powder
    200 gms Elephant's foot
    2 Pcs onions
    1 Pc ginger
    1 TSP garam masala
    1/2 TSP red chillies
    2 TBSP vegetable oil or ghee
    3 Pcs cloves
    Salt to taste

PROCESS

Clean rice thoroughly and soak in water. Heaten oil or ghee and fry small pieces of Elephant's foot in ghee/oil. Remove these pieces from oil/ghee. Fry cloves in ghee/oil and also onion pieces (chopped), pulverised ginger, garlic and green chillies. Thereafter, mix red chillies, turmeric, salt and garam masala. Now cook fried pieces of elephant's foot and shuffle 2-3 times with help of a large sized spoon. Lastly mix soaked rice (after removing water) and cook all the ingredients together.

ORANGE PULLAO

INGREDIENTS

2 cups rice
1 TSP salt
½ TSP black pepper
Green corriander leaves
1 cup orange juice (Fresh)
1 cup dry fruits
2 nos green chillies
1 TSP ghee

PROCESS

Wash rice and let it soak in water. Heaten ghee in a pan and crackle chopped green chillies and mix it with salt and rice and let the contents fry for sometime, whereafter put in 3 cups of water and let the contents cook (but not fully cooked, at this stage).

Mix black pepper with orange juice and mix with half cooked rice and place on slow fire. In all probability rice will fully get cooked after 4-5 minutes. Then remove from fire or put out flame/ fire. Spread dry fruits and chopped corriander leaves and enjoy this tasty preparation.

Rice Chowmien

INGREDIENTS

    200 gms Rice

    100 gms onions

    100 gms tomatoes

    1 TSP garam masala

    ½ TSP turmeric powder

    2 TSP vinegar

    1 TSP soya sauce

    ½ TSP cumin

    50 gms French beans

    5 gms cablbage (finely chopped)

    ½ TSP red chillies (powder)

    ¼ TSP black pepper

    Salt to taste

    100 gms capsicum

PROCESS

Boil rice, adding salt to taste, and remove gruel. Finely chop capsicum, onion, French bean and tomato. Heaten oil in a stew pan, and crackle cumin seeds in the oil. Then fry onion in the oil. Pour in all the vegetables after beans have fried, including garam masala, and let the contents cook on slow fire. If necessary, sprinkle water.

When vegetables are half-baked, put in rice and thoroughly mix all the ingredients. Thereafter add vinegar and soya sauce and again mix with the help of a big spoon. This a delicious delicacy.

COCONUT PULLAO (II VARIETY)

INGREDIENTS

150 gms rice

1 Pc lemon

1/2 TSP salt

Green corriander leaves

1 Pc fresh coconut (raw)

1 TSP cumin

1 TSP butter

PROCESS

Cleanse rice and soak in water, drain out water from raw coconut and process chutively, grinding the white portion. Crackle cumin seeds and condement rice. Then add 275 gms of water and salt, and let it cook. When partly cooked, mix lemon juice and coconut water. When rice is fully cooked add and mix coconut chutni. Remove from fire and spread green corriander (chopped) leaves and serve.

BUTTER PULLAO (MAKHANI PULLAO)

INGREDIENTS

2 cups rice
1/2 cup butter
1 cup garam masala
1/2 cup fried cashew nuts
2 cups cheese (grated)
1 Pc onion
1/2 cup fried alwond (kernel)
Salt to taste (if necessary)

PROCESS

Cleanse rice and soak in water. Fry chopped (numied) onion in 2 TSP butter. Then fry rice, mix to cups of tea and add salt, garam masala and balance quantity of butter. Add also cheese and onion, and let the contents cook.

When the rice is half-leaked, let it be kept on slow fire. Spread rest of the ingredient on rice and it cook for 2-3 minutes (But cover the pan with a led) and then remove from fire finally garnish or spread fried almonds and cashewnuts and enjoy delectable taste of butter pullao.

ROSE PULLAO

INGREDIENTS

2 cups rice

1 cup asserted dry fruits

50 gms cardamoin seeds

2 TSP pure desi ghee

2 cups rose water

1 cup milk

1 cup sugar

PROCESS

Pour ghee in a pan and let it heaten, whereafter crackle cardamon seeds, and then put in thoroughly cleansed and washed rice (previously soaked in water). Fry rice and other contents for 2-3 minutes whereafter add rose water and milk and let the contents cook. When rice is about to dry up, add sugar. Now taper the flame ad spread menced dry fruits over it.

Palak Pullao (Spinach Pullao)

INGREDIENTS

- 250 gms spinach
- 50 gms onion
- 1/2 Pc ginger
- 1/2 TSP turmeric powder
- 1 TSP corriander
- 3 TSP oil
- 250 gms rice
- 3-4 cloves of garlic
- 1 Pc Tomalo
- 1/2 TSP red chillies
- 1/2 TSP garam masala
- 1 TSP cumin salt to taste

PROCESS

Cleanse rice and soak in water boil spinach and grind.

Slice onion, garlic, ginger and tomato into small pieces. Put oil in a pan and crackle cumin seed and fry ground spinach in oil. Now add all the masals and salt.

Pour 400 gms water in a pan and boil, adding rice. When rice is half-baked, remove from fire and remove gruel and mix spinach and let it remove on fire for 4-5 minutes when rice cooks properly, remove from fire.

II. Soth Indian Dishes

Rice Dosa

INGREDIENTS

> 1 cup rice
> 1 TSP corriander seeds oil
> 1 cup pulse of horse beam
> Salt to taste

PROCESS

Soak separately pulse of horse bean, rice and corriander seeds for 6 hours. Then remove water from all the contents and prepare a paste of each item separately. Now mix all the three ingredients and mix salt. Keep the mixed contents over night.

Next morning add hot water to the paste and prepare gruel for preparing dosas. Put a TSP of oil and a pinch of salt on the steel plate. When oil starts to crackle, cleanse the steel plate with a cloth piece.

Apply some oil the steel plate and put 2 TSP of paste thereon and spread (with a big spoon or bowel). Cover with a lid.

When dosa turns brownish from one side, reverse the side, when second side also gets brown, remove from the steel plate and serve with coconut sauce/jelly.

JAGGERY DOSA (GUR KA DOSA)

INGREDIENTS

> 1/2 cup pulverised rice flour
> 1/2 cup grated coconut
> 1/2 cup jaggery
> 1 cup fine flour/maidas
> 1 TSP powder of cardamon oil

PROCESS

Soak jaggery in hot water, when jaggery melts or fully liquifies, then sift/serve in a piece of cloth and mix maida and rice flour to it.

Mix some milk to the above mixture, alongwith powder of cardamon. Method of preparation is similar to the one detailed under 'Rice Dosa'.

MASALA DOSA

INGREDIENTS FOR DOSA

100 gms rice   *25 gms turmeric salt*

1/2 TSP turmeric   *25 gms sirse bean*

Curry leaves   *Corriander leaves oil.*

INGREDIENTS FOR SLUFFING IN DOSA

300 gms potatoes   *4 Pcs green chillies*

1 pinch asafoetida salt   *125 gms onion*

1/2 TSP oil   *1/2 TSP mustard*

PROCESS

Separately soak horse bean and rice in water for six hours. Thereafter remove the ingredients from water and grind separately. Mix both and reduce, and add salt to it. When you intend to make dosas, mix the ingredients and thoroughly shuffle so as to prepare a liquefied mixture. Boil potatoes and slice them into small pieces. Fry mustard and then put in onion (chopped). When both items assume brownish color Add. Turmeric, minced green chillies and again fry all the ingredients for another two minutes. Then add potatoes and salt. Soak turmeric in hot water and when it saftens extra it its juice and mix it and chopped corriander leaves with potatoes and fry. Place a flat steel plate on flame. Apply some oil to it and spread rice mixture over it which should be made circular with the help of a big spoon or a bowl (kalori). Splash on oil corner of dosa. When one side of dosa turns brown, turn upside down and let it also turn brown.

Stuff in potato mixture on dosa and fold roll it and fry till it becomes crispy. Serve with coconut sauce.

Coconut Idli (I Variety)

INGREDIENTS

> 1 cup rice
> Salt
> Sugar
> 1 grated coconut
> Oil

PROCESS

Cleanse rice and let it remain soaked in water for 6 hours where after remark it out of water and grind to fire paste form commonly known as peethe of dal or rice.

Mix grated coconut to the rice paste and again grind. Add salt to the vegultant content and let it remain as it is in the same position. Now prepare dosa as detailed earlier.

You can relish and serve this kind of dosa with butter, honey, butter, sugar, ghee or faggery.

RICE-SOOFI DOSA

(Dosa prepared from coarse ground flour Soofi and Rice)

INGREDIENTS

1/2 cup rice flour
1 cup fine flour of wheat (maida)
4 Pcs chopped green chillies
1 Pc coconut (small size)-grated
1 cup coarse ground flour (soofi)
2 Pcs onions finely chopped into small pieces
corriander (green) leaves
1/2 cup cashew nut (minced into small pieces)
Oil
Salt to taste

PROCESS

Mix flour of soofi, maida and rice and sift. Now add onion corriander, green chillies, cashew nut and salt to the above flour. First knead the flour by mixing requisite quantity of then. Again add water to prepare sulatile enmulsion. Cook like rice dosa, as indicated earlier.

Masala Idli

INGREDIENTS

250 gms rice
11/2 coconut
2 Nos green chillies
Salt
Oil
25 gms grain pulse
1 Pc onion
50 gms Turmeric
1/2 red chilly powder

PROCESS

Soak pulse and rice separately for 2 hours and thereafter grind both the contents. Mix coconut (grated) and turmeric liquide and grind again (Note: Turmeric should be soaked in water to extract its juice). Add lemon, green chillies corriander, salt and chilly powder to the gruel and prepare a condensed gruel of the thick consitancy. Take a few bowls and apply some oil inside each bowl. Now fill in the bowls to 3/4th capacity and place in a pain in which water should be put to such a level that the bowls do not immerse fully so that water level should measure upto 3/4th capacity of the levels (so that water doesn't gain entry). Place the pan on fire, after covering the same with a cover. Let the idlies cook in the steam generated. When fully cooked, remove idlies from the bowls and place in plates of steel or chinaware and serve with curd, sambhar or coconut sauce.

Coconut Idli (II Variety)

INGREDIENTS

    1 cup half boiled sice
    1 cup grated coconut
    1 TSP mustord seeds
    1 Pc onion (chopped)
    curry leaves
    Oil
    1 TBSP grain dal (Chane ki dal)
    1 TBSP horse bean
    1 Pc Red chilly
    2 Pcs green chillies
    Salt

PROCESS

Let rice remain soaked in water for 6 hours, whereafter grind it with coconut to fine emulsion form.

Heaten a TSP of oil add mustard, horse bean pulse (Dal) in oil. When pulse turns rosy or brownish, add onion, green chillies and curry leaves. Remove from fire, when onion pieces turn brownish after frying. Mix rice powder and coconut to the above mixutre and prepare mixture of thick consistency. Then process idlies, as suggested for processing Masala Idli.

Sweet (Plain) Idli

INGREDIENTS

1 cup rice

1/2 cup Jaggery

1 cup horse beam pulse

1 TSP cardamon powder

PROCESS

Soak faggery in a bowl, putting a cup of water when it dessolves fully, filter the same. Soak rice and pulse separately for 7 bvurs after which remove water and grend separately. Now mix. Jaggry liquid with composite mixture of rice and pulse. Keep it at some warm place, for 2 hour. The contents should be filled in an idly stand and let the same cook under steam.

Plain Idli

INGREDIENTS

2 cups rice

1 cup pulse of horse bean

Salt

A pinch of sod-bi-carb

PROCESS

Soak pulse and rice separately for 6 hours, after which remove from water and grind separately. Mix soda, salt and some water. Prepare a mixture and let it remain overnight in the ulinsil.

In the morning prepare take Masala Dosa idli and serve along-with smbhar.

Veg Idli

INGREDIENTS

2 cups rice

1/4 cup horse-bean pulse

50 gms green peas

25 gms cabbage

1/4 cup grain flour

1 pinch soda bicarli

Salt

1 Pc coconut

1 Pc potato

1 Pc carrot

1 TSP cumin

1 Pc onion

2 TSP grated coconut

1 Pc ginger

PROCESS

Boil all the vegetables and chop into small pieces. Soak pulse and rice separately and then let these remain soaked for 6 hours, whereafter grind each other separately and them mix.

Grind coconut and extract its juice (milk) add ginger, cumin and clullies to vegetables. Mix rice, pulse, coconut, green corriander leaves, onion salt and soda to coconut milk, alongwith all the vegetables and prepare a mixture.

Fill the said mixture in the Idli. Stand and cook under steam and Serve with sambhar.

KOTHAPPAM

INGREDIENTS

- 125 gms rice
- 1 Pc onion (chopped)
- 1/2 Pc ginger
- Salt to taste
- 50 gms horse bean pulse
- 4 Nos green chillies
- Green Corriander
- Ghee

PROCESS

Let rice and pulse remain soaked in water an overnight. Next morning remove the contents from water and grind and the paste should be kept, as it is, for 24 hourse.

Mix salt and spices and prepare a mixture. Place a steel plate on fire and spread mixture thereon in circular shape. When one side turns brown, turn it upside down. Spread some ghee on the corner and let the other side also assume dark brown colour.

Chabali / Chakali

INGREDIENTS

1/2 cup rice
1/2 cup kidney bean (pulse)
1 TSP cumin
1/2 TSP red chillies
1 cup grain pulse
1/2 cup pigeon pea
2 TBSP ghee
Salt to taste

PROCESS

Fry rice in a frying pan (in ghee) and grind finely. Grind all the spices and mix with rice, to prepare a thick paste, adding requisite quantity of water. Heaten ghee or oil in a pan or stewpan. Process Cakes out of the mixture (paste) and fry till they assume golden colour.

Now, put all the cakes in such a ulinsil where air cannot let in, that is with an air tight lid.

Kuzal

INGREDIENTS

4 cups rice flour
1 TSP black pepper
1 TBSP butter
1 pinch of asifoetida
1/4 cup horse bean flour
1 TBSP cumin powder
2 TBSP til seeds
Salt to taste

PROCESS

Grind all the spices in water and mix with flour of rice and horse bean and thoroughly churn the ingredients. Fry til seeds in a stewpan. Process rounded flat cakes out of the mixture and cover with til seeds.

Heaten oil in a stewpan, when oil heatens then taper the flame and fry the cakes on slow fire in the oil.

When all the cakes are fried, let them cool. Now place in an air-tight utensil. These cakes are known as 'Kuzal'.

Akaki Vada (of Mysore Variety)

INGREDIENTS

> 500 gms rice (flour)
> 1 TSP cumin seeds
> 4 green corriander
> 1 bunch of corriander leaves
> Oil
> Salt to taste
> 4 Nos green chillies
> 125 gms Urad ki dal

PROCESS

Thoroughly clean and wash the rice and let it dry in the sun, where after it should be reduced to powder form. Soak dal in water for a few hours and drain out water and then grind (by mixing with rice powder) to smooth and thick paste, mixing all the spices also. Process Voind Vadas out of this mixture and place on a wet clothe. Thereafter deeply fry in oil of til until they float to the surface. Drain out oil from all the Vadas.

Serve Akki Vada and also enjoy yourself its delicious taste.

Pani Pooly (Mangalove)

INGREDIENTS

    200 gms rice
    2 TBSP sugar
    1/2 Pc coconut
    Ghee or oil
    Cardamon
    Sugar to taste

PROCESS

Clean rice and soak in water for blours, after which remove from water (but do not drain out water) and grind to fine paste form and mix sugar and salt. Prepare a mixture of this consistency and mix grated coconut with it.

Spread oil on a flat steel/iron plate (Tewa). Process thin dosas with the help of a bowl or spoon. It should be served with Rasua.

METHOD TO PROCESS RASUA

Mix faggery with liquid content of two coconut pieces when faggery is fully dissolved in coconut water, add powder of cardamon.

Such Pani-Pooly tastes deliciously if eaten with a saltish chani.

VIPATTU

INGREDIENTS

1 cup rice flour
1 TSP ginger powder
2 TSP roasted chana
Salt to taste
1/2 TSP sugar (powdered)
2 TBSP groundnut sees
1 TSP Powder of red chillies
Oil

PROCESS

Make a soft dough by mixing rice; salt, sugar, and red chillies powder. Also palverise roasted black grain and ground nut.

Heaten ghee or oil in a stev pan. Place mixture on a wet cloth and compress from both sides. Mix powdered compound of ground nut and grains and fry. When the contents assume golden colour, remove from fire. Now you can eat and serve it hot.

CHAKRAI PONGAL

INGREDIENTS

    500 gms rice
    1 litre milk
    50 gms raisin
    1/2 cup Jaggery
    1 TSP powdered cardamon
    1 cup moon ki dal
    200 gms ghee
    1/2 TSP Nutinif (Jaiphal)
    50 gms cashew nuts

PROCESS

Cut cashew nuts into small pieces and wash raisns in water.

Heaten ghee or oil in a pan; wash rice and dal and fry them in ghee. Mix milk to the contents and shuffle and then let it cook.

When del and rice soften add faggery, nutinif and cardawon and let it cook on slow fire. When faggery fully gell mixed with rice and rice gets fully cooked, add raisins and cashew nut.

Coconut Rice

INGREDIENTS

2 cups boiled rice

1 phinch of asafoetida

1 cup urad ki dal

Curry leaves

1 TSP mustard

Salt to taste

1/4 cup grited coconut

50 gms fried cashew nuts

4 Nos green chillies

1 TSP chana ki dal

2 Nos red chillies

Coconut oil

PROCESS

Heaten 4 TBSP coconut oil in pan and put in mustard and asafoetida and fry the same. Then add red chilly and dal also. When the contents redden add coconut, green chillies and curry leaves. Continue to fry until coconut turns red. Now add rice and shuffly thoroughly.

When rice fully cooks, add cashewnut pieces.

VEN PONGAL

INGREDIENTS

250 gms rice
1 TSP black pepper
1 Pc ginger
25 gms fried raisens
Salt to tast
1 cup moong dal
1 TSP cumin
50 gms fried cashew nuts
Curry leaves
Ghee

PROCESS

Heaten 8 TBSP of ghee in a pan and fry cumin and black pepper in ghee.

When cumin (seads) are fully ried, add dal and fry. Then add rice, curry leaves, ginger, salt and fry.

Put in so much water that it stands 1/2 inch above the level of rice. Cover with a lid and reduce heat to sun mering. Cook rice until it is fully dry and tender.

Garnish with raisins and cashew nuts and serve hot.

AKHATA (KERALA)

INGREDIENTS

> 2 cup rice
> 1/2 cup ghee
> TSP corriander
> 50 gms gralid
> Coconut (Dried)
> 250 gms saggery (finely pourded)
> 50 gms cashew nut (fried)
> 50 gms raisins (fried)
> Salt to taste

PROCESS

Put in 4 cups of water in a pan, add rice and cook. When rice fully cook add faggery and pounded corriander to it. Let the contents contents until faggery fully mixed.

There after put in some ghee and fry for two minutes and remove from fire when fully cooked and fried.

While serving add fried coconut, cashew nut and raisings and shuffle thoroughly.

RICE WAFERS

INGREDIENTS

1 cup rice flour
1 TBSP foppy seeds
Salt to taste
3 TBSP sago
1 TSP cumin

PROCESS

Boil sago in 4 cups of water. When sago melts, mix rice flour and cook. Add some more water, if necessary.

When the contents get fully cooked spread a mustin cloth over the pan, hold it tightly and filter. Then add cumin and salt. Shuffle thoroughly and process then and rounded wafers.

Place the same under sun and when the wafers heaten and dry up fill in the same in a container and tightly close with a lid whenever you need to eat, fry a few pieces in ghee or oil.

APPAM

INGREDIENTS

100 gms rice
1/2 Pc coconut 1 grated
Ghee
100 gms Jaggery
1/4 TSP red chillies
Milk

PROCESS

Wash rice with water, let it dry, where after grind the same so as to produce a paste. Mix jaggery to it and again grind. If necessary add some quantity of jaggery and knead to thick consistency. Then put in powder of red chillies and grated coconut and thoroughly stuffle.

Heaten gheen in a stewpan. Process rounded laddoos out of the mixture and fry till they assume rosy/brown colour.

Appam is relished and enjoyed when served hot.

RAS BARA

INGREDIENTS

600 gms Rice

25 gms Jaggery

Ghee

1 Pc coconut (soft)

Salt

PROCESS

Grind fresh coconut and extract its milk. Wash rice and let it dry. When fully dried, grind it finely an filter properly.

Thoroughly shuffle rice flour, salt and jaggery in coconut milk and mix. Process small rounded pieces from this content in the shape and size of a lemon.

Flatten the rounded pieces with the helf of your palm and keep on placing upon a banana leave and fry these pieces in ghee. Now fry in ghee in a stew pan until it turn rosy.

CLUTRANA

INGREDIENTS

1/2 kg rice
1/2 TSP turmeric
1/2 Pc coconut
Green corriander leaves
5 Nos green chillies
Chana ki Dal and Urad ki Dal [as per taste and need]
1 TSP ground nut
1 TSP mustard
2 Nos lemon
2 TBSP oil
Curry leaves

PROCESS

Wash rice and cook thorougly. Heaten oil in a pan. Put in mustard, dal of Urad and Chana, ground nut, green chillies, turmeric curry leaves and chopped corriander leaves and fry. After frying put in rice. Add also salt and mix all the ingredients thoroughly.

Extract juice of lemon and mix with rice shuffle all the contents. Last of all mix graled coconut and enjoy the delicacy.

CHAKALI

INGREDIENTS

 1 cup chana ki dal
 1/2 cup moon ki dal
 Oil
 1/2 cup rice
 1/2 TSP red chillies

PROCESS

Deep fry rice and both the pulses till the contents turn brown and then grind the contents. Prepare a liquid mixture by blending all the spices.

Heaten oil in a stewpan and reduce the contents in the form of round shape /Chakali (— that is on the shape of a chakala on your process loaves/ Chapatis and fry, where after put it in a pan, having a lid, which is air tight. Cover with lid.

Masala Poori

INGREDIENTS

100 gms rice (pardied)
Green chillies
1 TSP corriander
25 gms roasted black grain
Tamarevd juice / extract
1 No. onion
1/2 TSP red chillies
1/2 TSP amchoor (dried powder of mangoes)
1/2 TSP salt

PROCESS

Mix all the ingredients as is done while processing 'Bhelpoori'. Now mix tamarevd liquid or sprinkle a few drops of mustard oil. Mix parclied rice. Shuffle all the ingredients.

This preparation can be eaten with tea.

Mysore Kheer

INGREDIENTS

250 gms milk
30 gms chana ki dal
25 gms cardamon
25 gms raisins
50 gms rice
25 gms cashew nut
1/2 green coconut
1/2 TBSP ghee

PROCESS

First cook rice and pulse in a cooker and let in cool. Then add milk to it (after cooling) and then again place on fire and keep on shuffling with a large sized spoon.

When Kheer is ready, remove cooker from fire and then mix cardamon, green, dry fruit is cardamon and grated coconut.

RICE KHEER

INGREDIENTS

1 kg milk
25 gms dry coconut (golanarial)
25 Nos almond /Kernels
1 TSP rose water of kevada (Pandanies, fragrant flowers' essence)
100 gms sugar
75 grains rice (basmati)
25 gms ghee
25 gms sipida (chiramfi)
Saffron
25 gms raisins
10 Pcs cardamon

PROCESS

Heaten ghee in a pan. Fry rice until it turns rosy, and then remove from fire.

Put milk in a pan and let it beaten and cook on slow fire.

When kheer gets thickened add sugar. Kheer will liquefy after putting in sugar, hence let it remove on fire for some time.

Dissolve saffron flakes in 1/2 cup of water and put in saffron liquid and all the dry fruits and remove the utensil from fire.

When kheer turns cold, sprinkle kevada and rose water.

NARVAL KE PEETHEY

INGREDIENTS

500 gms rice
25 gms pestachies
25 gms raisins
100 gms dry coconut
25 gms cashew nut
25 gms almond kernel
10 gms cardamon
500 gms sugar

PROCESS

Wash rice and let it dry in the heat of sun. But, before that let the rice remain soaked in water for an hour. When rice gets dried, grind to fine powder form.

Boil 250 gms of water in a pan and pour in rice and whisk with a large spoon. When entire water content evaporates/dries up, remove from fire.

Boil water in a separate pan and wrap its top with a muslin cloth (not tight). Place all the coconut rolls and let them cook under steam and cover with a lid, and to generate more steam keep on light fire. When the coconut rolls get fully cooked, remove them from fire and put in another pan.

In a stewpan prepare syrup of sugar and put the coconut rolls in the syrup.

Whenever you eat it, remove the rolls from syrup and enjoy eating the coconut rolls.

RICE RASGULLAS

INGREDIENTS

125 gms rice flour
1 kg milk
500 gms sugar
1 pinch citric acid

PROCESS

Place milk in a pan and add a pinch of citric acid and then boil milk. When milk ferments filter out water content through a seeve/ muslin cloth and keep it aside. Mix rice flour with 'Chana' (Cheese) and knead/ mix thoroughly. Then process small rolls out of the mixture.

Put water and sugar in a stew pan and prepare sugar syrup in which rolls should be put in and let them cook. When the rolls have so flewd, remove form fire. Let the rolls cool, whereafter enjoy eating tasty rasgullas.

III. Meat Preparation

Biryani

INGREDIENTS

750 gms rice
1 kuoli garbe
1 No cannamon
50 gms Pilmond (kernel)
Salt
1 kg weight chicken murgi
8 Nos black pepper
1/2 TSP cumin
50 gms raisins
Red chillies

250 gms curd
8 Nos cloves
1/2 TSP cumin (white)
250 gms ghee
3 gms saffron
250 gms onion
1 TSP corriander
4 Nos eggs
4 Nos cardamon

PROCESS

Clean chicken (hen) and process small eatable pieces. Prepare round pieces, grind garlic. Pound all the spices, except cloves and cinnamon. Fry onion pieces to deep brown colour and remove from stewpan, when the pieces cool, grind finely on a pastel. Put in cloves and cinnamon in ghee, add chicken pieces and fry on slow fire till they turn red. Mix salt and curd and add to chicken pieces. When curd fully gets absorbed, add pulp of garlic and spices. Sprinkle water and fry to such an extent that pieces get half-melted. Soak rice for half-an-hour and the boil. When rice is on verge of baking remove gruel and add some cold water. Spread rice on surface of an open mouthed utersil. Spread half quantity of chicken pieces over rice. Again spread rice over these pieces and then spread another layer of rest of the chicken pieces. Again spread a layer of rice over the pieces. Let the contents boil on slow fire. Boil eggs and cut small round shaped pieces. Soak almonds and then peel off the skin. Fry raisins in ghee. When biryani is fully ready garnish with almonds, raisins, egg pieces and saffron.

AKABARI MURAG-BHAAT

INGREDIENTS

1 No hen	300 gms ghee/oil
8 Pcs garlic	1 kg rice
1/2 TSP red chillies	250 gms green peas
2 cups chicken slack	3 Pcs onion
250 gms tomato	Bay leaves
1 gm saffron	6 Nos cloves

PROCESS

Clean hen and cut into 6-8 pieces and then clean with salt mixed water. Apply (marinate) red chillies and salt over the pieces and let it remain so far 10 minutes. Heaten ghee in a utensil (with thick surface) and fry chicken pieces and remove when pieces turn slightly red. Again fry the pieces and remove when fully red. Keep the fried pieces, in a dish, separately. Fry onion, garlic, ginger in the same ghee. Wash rice and mix with the fried ingredients. When rice turns light rosy, put in chopped tomato pieces. Now add chicka pieces (already fried) and saffron. Thoroughly shuffle chicken pieces with a large spoon and cook until it is half cooked.

You can also utilise an oven for the purpose. Put peas in some water and cover with a lid. When peas soften, drain out water and garnish over the above preparation serve hot.

MUGHLAI-CHICKEN PULLAO

INGREDIENTS

4 cups rice

4 Pcs onion

1 TSP carom seeds (ajwain)

100 gms cloppe and
fried almond kernel

500 gms basmati rice

1/2 TSP cumin

10 Nos cardamon

3 gms saffron

2 TSP red chillies

1 chicken

2 cups green peas

1 Pc cinnamon

50 gms ginger

2 TSP corriander

200 gms roundly
sliced onion pieces

18 Nos black pepper

12 Nos cloves

1 TSP jurineric

PROCESS

Grind ginger, garlic, chillies, corriander, turmeric, cumin to fine paste form. Heaten some quantity of ghee and fry sliced onion rounds. Then add chicken pieces and garam masala (whole) and its powder and fry till the ingredients turn brown. Add 2 cups of water and cover, with a lid. Churn curd and dissolve saffron in it and then put in the pan. After cooking the contents for 10 minutes, remove from fire. Now heaten ghee and fry rest of the spices. Add balance quantity of onion pieces and fry until red. Requisite quantity of water should be added alongwith a TSP of salt and let it bake on slow fire. Thereafter, spread a layer of cooked rice on a dish. Then spread chicken pieces and follow this course until stock of rice and chicken pieces exhausts.

Garnish with sliced pieces of almonds.

PEAS-CHICKEN AND RICE

INGREDIENTS

4 cups rice

1 chicken

2 cups green peas

Ghee

500 gms B

Salt

1 bulk of garlic

6 Pc onion

5 green chillies

1 TSP ajwain leaves (celery)

1 bulk of garlic

Tomato

8 Nos cloves

Eggs

PROCESS

Clean the chicken, wash with water, cut into pieces and boil.

First prepare tomato souce grind 1/2 kg tomatoes in a mixture. Grind onions, cloves, garlic, green chillies and fry, adding on salt and tomato to it. Tomatoes will soften after a few minutes which should be removed from fire and kept aside. Deep fry chicken pieces in ghee and keep them apart, after removing from ghee.

Fry rice until it is pink. Then add peas, salt, turmeric, powder of red chillies and then fry the contents. When all the said ingredients get fully fried, put it chicken pieces until entire water content evaporates (dries). The put the said contents in an oven, where it should be kept for 7-8 minutes.

When all the contents melt/soften, spread tomatoes in the centre of dish. Spread chicken, rice peas etc. all around tomatoes. On the corner spread tomato sauce.

Garnish with celery leaves and boiled and chopped pieces of eggs.

Muglai-mug-kalegi-rice

INGREDIENTS

500 gms kaleji (lever of chicken)

1 bulk of garlic

1/2 cup cheese

4 Pcs tomato

6 TSP butter

1 TSP red chillies

2 cups rice

2 Pcs onion

2 cups chicken stalk

1 gm saffron

4 TSP ghee

PROCESS

Heaten 3 cups each of ghee and butter in a pan. Fry onion on slow fire and, when they turn pinkish, and rice to it and fry for 3-4 minutes. When rice fully fry, add salt and stalk to it and cover with a lid. Dissolve saffron in minutes and, after 10 minutes add to cooked rice.

Boil liver, ginger and salt. Then chop into small pieces.

When rice get fully cooked, remove from fire. Then fry liver tomato and cheese in some quantity of ghee and spread over rice. Add balance quantity of ghee and butter to the above, keep in an oven at 360°F.

If you do not have an over, place some burning charcoal over the lid and then let the contents cook.

YAKLINI-CHAWAL-MURG

INGREDIENTS (FOR YAKLINI)

1 kg meat cinnamon
(6" long piece)
1 TSP green chillies
10 cups water

6 No. cloves of garlic
3 Nos green chillies
4 Nos cloves
Salt

INGREDIENTS (FOR RICE)

250 gms rice
1 Pc cinnamon
1 TSP powder of red chillies
1 TSP cumin
4 Nos cloves
8 TSP ghee

2 TSP turmeric
2 Pc cardamon
50 gms onion
(rounded pieces)
3 Nos Bay leaves

PROCESS

Wash meat thoroughly and chop into pieces. All the mutton pieces and spices be boiled in water clean rice and soak in water. Heaten ghee in a pan and first of all, onion pieces. When onion pieces turn brown, fry other spices. Now add rice and fry properly.

Filter/sieve yaklini and add to rice when it (rice) turns pinkish.

When rice get half-baked, put in mutton pieces and cover the pan with a lid.

Let the contents bake on slow fire. When rice bake completely and water evaporates, put the contents in a dish and decorate with then silver foil is on the top.

VEG-MUTTON-BIRYANI

INGREDIENTS

    500 gms meat

    250 gms potatoes

    100 gms peas

    300 gms ghee

    125 gms curd

    125 gms onions

    500 gms rice

    2 TSP garam masala

    1 TSP red chillies (powder)

    3 gms saffron

    6 Nos cardamon

    1/2 TSP turmeric (powder)

PROCESS

Slice onions into round pieces. Peel ginger and garlic. Boil potatoes, peas and salt. Fry onion pieces in ghee until they turn pink. Fry meat in the same ghee. When meat assumes pinkish. Colour, add paste of garlic and ginger and fry thoroughly. Fried and grinded onion should be added to the above material. Now add red chilly powder, turmeric and garam masala. Put in requisite quantity of water so that meat melts and softens. Boil rice and mix with meat.

Noorjahani Biryani

INGREDIENTS

- 1 kg meat
- 100 gms onions
- 2 cups curd
- 1 TSP red chillies
- 1 TSP black pepper
- 6 Nos caramon
- Salt
- 500 gms rice
- 1 bulk of ginger
- 2 Pcs cinnomon
- 4 Nos bay leaves
- 6 Nos cloves

PROCESS

Heaten ghee in a pan and roast/fry all the spices. Cut onion into round shaped pieces and fry. Then add salt, chillies, corriand sugar and fry all the ingredients for 5 minutes. Add 2-3 cups of water, cover with a lid and cook.

Cook rice in another pan by adding ghee. When rice turns brown add masala to it. Separate 1/2 quantity of masala. Cook rice on slow fire.

When rice bake fully, put in fried pieces of meat and 1/2 masala. Then let the contents remain on slow fire on charcoal fire. When all the ingredients are fully cooked, remove the pan from fire.

SHAHI-PULLAO

INGREDIENTS

1/2 kg chicken lemons	750 gms rice
100 gms onion	1/2 TSP saffron
12 Nos cardomon	25 Nos fried almonds
1 TSP red chillies	Salt
1/2 kg meat	8 TSP ghee
500 gms curd	3 Nos bay leaves
18 Nos black pepper	1 TSP corriander powder
1 bulk of ginger	

PROCESS

Grind garlic ginger turmeric, corriander and red chillies. Pour 4 TSP ghee in a pan and fry onion pieces. Then put in half quantity of chicken and meat in it and keep on frying till it turns pink.

Put in 2 cups of water, cover with a lid and let it cook. When cooks fully add churned curd and dessolved saffron (in curd) and keep the utensil on fire 10 minutes, after which remove the same from fire.

Pour ghee in another pan. First fry bay leaves and then fry onion (sliced) pieces.

Then put in rice to the above and fry the same until it gets fully pinkish. Add salt and water (as per requirement) and let it cook on slow fire.

When rice bake fully spread a layer in a dish and then it should be covered with meat. This way spread first rice and then meat, so on and so forth.

Pullao Zafrani

INGREDIENTS

500 grams boiled chops
250 gms boiled meat
8 Nos boiled eggs
8 Nos raisins
8 Nos pistachio (slices)
3 cups curd
2 TSP saffron (dissolved in milk)
500 gms boiled rice
500 gms ghee
500 gms onions (sheed)
8 Nos almonds (grinded)
3 No bay leaves
2 Pcs garlic (paste)
1/2 cup milk
Salt

PROCESS

Heaten ghee in a pan and fry boiled eggs. Then fry bay leaves and remove 1/2 quantity of ghee. Fry in (heated) ghee garlic, ginger, and put in chops and meat in the same ghee, until it gets deep fried. Then remove from fire. Now add curd, salt, garam masala, cumin, black pepper, raisins, eggs, pistachio etc. and shuffly thoroughly. Spread rice evenly over the above contents and mix rest of ghee, milk and saffron. Shuffle all the ingredients thoroughly and cook on slow fire for 20 minutes.

BIRYANI NIZAMI

INGREDIENTS

2 cups boiled rice

250 gms ghee

1/2 TSP saffron

8 Nos red chillies

6 Nos cloves

500 gms boiled pieces
of meat

1/4 TSP orange colour
(edible variety)

2 Nos green chillies

Salt

500 gms boiled and fried potatoes
and green corriander

3 TSP milk

1 Pc cinnamon

3 Nos cardamon

250 gms curd (fully churned)

500 gms extracted juice
of onions

1/2 Pc ginger

6 Nos Black pepper

PROCESS

Finely grind all the spices, ginger and garlic. Pulverase cardamon, cinnamon, cloves, black pepper and keep separately. Mix all the spices pieces of meat, salt, extract of onions, potatoes and fry in warmed ghee. After frying add rice to the above contents. Pour also saffron mixed milk and vouge colour.

Prepare a thick paste poin wheat flour place a lid over the pan and cover with this paste keep on light fire. Biryani will be ready for use with 10-20 minutes where after chopped corriander leaves should be spread over it.

BIRYANI BADSHAHI

INGREDIENTS

500 gms rice (boiled)

2 TBSP green corriander
   (chopped)

1 Pc ginger

1 Pc cinnamon

Salt

20 Pcs Almonds (menced)

2 TSP oil (Til oil)

1 TSP saffron

1 kg curd

3 TBSP lemon juice

4 Nos cardamon

2 bulb garlic

1 TSP green chillies
   (chopped)

250 gms milk

4 Nos onions (large sized)

4 Nos cloves

1 TSP red chillies (powdered)

6 cups water

PROCESS

Warm butter in a pan and fry onion pieces (chopped in circular form) until they turn pink. Dissolve saffron in water. Fry ginger, red chillies, garlic and almonds in butter. Add meat pieces to the contents and fry for 5 minutes. Pour in water and cook on slow fire. Put rice and salt in another pan and boil adding some water.

Churn curd and filter through a thin muslin cloth. Add some water to it. Then mix cloves, cardamon, cumin, meat, green chillies to curd. Then mix dissolved saffron and juice of lemon.

Spread a layer of rice on another pan. Then spread another layers of fried onions and pieces of meat. Thoroughly shuffle the ingredients. Heaten better and pour in the said pan and warm on slow fire, after closing mouth of the pan, for 10-15 minutes. Now Biryani Badshahi is ready for use.

KEEMA BIRYANI AND RICE

INGREDIENTS

500 gms rice
250 gms onion
6 Nos cloves
1 TSP cumin (white)
300 gms ghee
125 gms curd
250 gms lumps of keema
4 Nos cardamon
2 Pcs cinnamon
125 gms tomatoes
50 gms garlic
Salt

PROCESS

Clean rice and soak in water. Half quantity of onion should be sliced and other half should be grinded with garlic. Finely chop ginger and tomatoes. Pound 1/2 quantity of garam masala and other half portion should be retained as it is. Put 1/2 quantity of ghee in a pan and fry keema lumps. There after fry grinded onion garlic, tomatoes in the same ghee and fry thoroughly. Add garam masala and small quantity of water to it and remove from fire. Fry onion in rest of ghee. Then mix salt, garam masala and curd. When liquid content of curd dries up, add rice to it.

When rice gets half boiled, add keema lumps to it and cook on slow fire. When entire quantity of water diminishes, remove from fire and enjoy the tasty delicacy.

Fish Kefari

INGREDIENTS

250 gms fish
125 gms rice
1 egg
4 Nos cloves
1/2 TSP black pepper
1/2 TSP garam masala
Green corriander
Salt
1 Pc onion
2 Nos Cardamon
1/2 TSP red chillies
3 TBSP ghee
2 Pcs onion slices

PROCESS

Cleanse fish properly, boil and slice into small pieces.

Cleanse rice and boil. Fry onion slices in warm ghee (in a pan) and remove from pan.

Fry fisrt garam masala and then add fish pieces and rice to it and shuffly thoroughly. Boil egg and chop into slices and spread over fish and rice in circular form. Finally garnish with chopped green corriander leaves.

FISH PULLAO

INGREDIENTS

250 gms fish

1 Pc ginger

4 Nos cardamon (large)

4 Nos bay leaves

Salt

2 bulks of garlic

12 Nos cloves

4 Cardamon (small)

125 gms ghee

50 gms onion

1/2 TSP powdered
 black pepper

1 TSP turmeric

250 gms rice

2 bundles green corriander

1 Pc cinnamon

1 TSP red chillies

PROCESS

Clean fish and slice into small pieces clean rice and soak in water. Chop onions into circular pieces. Fry all the spices excepting black pepper, cloves, cardamon and bay leaves. Pour ghee in a pan and fry onion pieces. Put in other spices and again fry. Then put in fish pieces and let them also fry. After frying, let the contents cook.

Warm ghee in another utensil and fry cinnamon, cloves, bay leaves and cardamon, after which add rice to such contents and fry rice thoroughly. After clung this much, spread fish upon rice and close with a lid.

Cook on slow fire. This way both rice and fish will soften. When entire water evaporates, remove the pan from fire and them sprinkle green corriander leave upon it.

Japani Pullao

INGREDIENTS

    2 Eggs
    25 gms sesamum seeds
    10 gms cumin
    250 gms rice
    50 gms onion
    Salt

PROCESS

Thoroughly clean rice and soak in water shuffle eggs and prepare an omellete chop onion into circular pieces. Heaten ghee in a pan and fry/roast cumin then add onion pieces, and till and fry until the contents turn rosy. Drain out water from rice. Mix rice and fried onion and after frying for some time, add salt and water (in such a quantity that rice soften). Spread rice on a plate and then garnish it with pieces of omellete.

CHINESE PULLAO

INGREDIENTS

500 gms rice

2 eggs

125 gms carrots (boiled)

125 gms green onions

125 gms ghee

125 gms chicken (boiled)

125 gms (lower portion of cauliflower)

3 Nos green chillies

PROCESS

Boil rice in water and add salt, when the rice is boiled upto 2/3rd capacity, keep the same aside. Separately boil chicken pieces and vegetables.

Warm ghee in a pan and put chopped vegetables, chicken pieces and chopped green chillies.

When vegetable and chicken pieces get roasted put in egg contents and stir briskly. Then add rice to it and comprise.

Rice will soften after 10-15 minutes, where after remove the pan from fire.

MEAT PULLAV

INGREDIENTS

500 gms rice
300 gms ghee
6 cloves of garlic
1 TSP garam masala
1/2 TSP black pepper
1 TSP cumin
1 TSP corriander
2 TSP turmeric
500 gms goat's meat
250 gms onion
25 gms garlic
6 Nos cloves
1 Pc cinnamon
4 Nos cardamon
1 TSP red chillies
Salt

PROCESS

Put meat pieces in a pan in hot water. Add salt, garlic, corriander, garam masala (whole) and ginger and then cook, water quantity should be sufficient only to let meat pieces immerse, and water should disappear and meat pieces soften or melt. Waram ghee in another pan and roast garam masala and onion in ghee. Having done so, put in rice and cover the pan with a lid let the contents cook on slow fire.

When rice cook fully, add to it pieces of meat and shuffle thoroughly. Serve hot.

Murga-Pullao

INGREDIENTS

1 kg chicken	300 gms ghee
50 gms garlic	100 gms onion
4 Nos cardamon	1 TSP cumin (white)
2 TSP red chillies	750 gms rice
50 gms garlic	1 TSP red chillies
1 TSP cumin (black)	2 Pcs cinnamon
2 TSP corriander	Green corriander leaves

PROCESS

Soak rice in water.

Clean the chicken and refrigerate for 24 hours. There after chop chicken into pieces and put in boiling water. Simultaneously also add garlic, ginger and half quantity of garam masala. Quantity of water should be such that a litre quantity of water remains even after meat pieces have soften. Now cook on slow fire. When chicken meal (pieces) fully soften and 'Yakhani' is also ready, remove from fire.

Warm ghee in another pan and fry onion and balance quantity of garlic. Fry until it turns brown and add chicken pieces and fry them also to brown colour. If Yakhani is inadquate, add more water. When Yakhani gets fully boiled, add rice and cover pan with a led.

When the entire preparation is ready remove the pan from fire and sprinkle cumin seeds.

Jheenga Pullao (Prawn Fish Pullao)

INGREDIENTS

1 kg prawn fish

1 TSP cumin (white)

2 TSP garam masala

750 gms rice

150 gms onion

4 Nos cardamon

1 TSP red chillies

50 gms ginger

2 Pcs cinnamon

Soyat leaves

2 bulks of garlic

8 Nos cloves

2 TSP corriander
  seeds (whole)

1 TSP cumin (black)

2 TSP turmeric

300 gms ghee

1 TSP black peper

Corriander (green leaves)

Salt

PROCESS

Cleanse prawn fish and wash with salt-mixed water. Keep it aside so that water content gets drained out.

Clean rice and soak in water. Warm ghee in a pan, cut soya leaves and put them ghee along with garam masala and roast thoroughly, after which put in prawn's pieces and let it cook on slow fire.

When prawn starts releasing water, raise fire temperature. When water dries fully, roast on slow fire.

When prawn softens, add rice and let the contents cook. Remove from fire when cooked fully.

Pullao of Meat Lumps (Bariyani)

INGREDIENTS

500 gms rice

250 gms white gourd (1 petha)

250 grains urad ki dal (pulse of horse bean) and all the ingredients mentioned under Murg-Pullao

PROCESS

Soak horse-bean (pulse) in water and let it remain soaked overnight. Next morning grind horse-bean to paste form. Grate white gourd and mix with paste of horse-bean. Add salt, chillies, garam masala (whole) and process lumps. If you wish you can procure such lumps from the market also and use.

Put a liter water in a pan and add meat pieces, salt and garam masala to prepare 'Yakhani'. Warm ghee in another pan and remove meat pieces out of yakhani and roast. Roast lumps of meat also.

When lumps soften, add rice and yakhani. Let the contents cook. Remove from fire when the contents get fully cooked.

EGG AND MEAT PULLAO

INGREDIENTS

500 gms rice

6 eggs

500 gms meat + all other in gredients which have been indicated earlier for processin 'Meat Pullao'

PROCESS

According to the process explained earlier, for processing Yakhani, prepare Yakhani from 250 gms meat and keep the same separately.

Boil eggs and divert them from its outer shell and cut into 4 pieces each. Fry in ghee until the egg pieces turn deep red. Add salt and some quantity of garam masala and fry thoroughly.

Put garam masala in ghee, mix rice and condiment the contents. Then add yakhani to it and cook.

When rice fully ripes spread a layer of keema. Spread another layer of eggs over keema. Sprinkle green corriander over the lest layer.

CHEESE ANIMAL

INGREDIENTS

    500 gms rice
    50 gms cheese
    1/2 TSP sesamum (Til)
    1/2 TSP wheat flour
    200 gms butter
    1 Egg
    1/2 TSP poppy seeds
    2 TSP milk

PROCESS

Mix flour and salt in a pan. Shuffle ghee and butter thoroughly and then add cheese to it. Now thoroughly knead flour in the said ingredients. Shuffle egg in milk and mix.

Give animal's shapes to the above mixture and besmear poppy seeds and sesamum (seeds) all over them, and place in an oven for 15 minutes for warming purpose.

Now cheese animal is ready for use.

CHICKEN KONJEY

INGREDIENTS

150 gms rice
2 Nos green onion
1 Pc ginger

250 gms chicken
1 kg chicken stalk
1 TSP salt

PROCESS

Slice chicken into small pieces. Place chicken stalk on slow fire for boiling. Wash rice, add salt and boil. When fully boiled, add rice to chicken stalk. Add finely chopped onion and garlic and boiled and sliced chicken to it. Serve hot.

PORK FORD RICE

INGREDIENTS

150 gms rice (boiled)
2 Pc green onion
1/4 TSP ajeeri omoto
100 gms pork (ready)
4 bulks garlic
½ TSP powder of black
   pepper

100 gms hen
2 eggs
Salt to taste
3 TSP oil
1 TSP soya souce

PROCESS

Deep fry chopped gren onion in warm ghee. Now fry chopped garlic. Shuffle eggs and add to the fried contents. Thoroughly whistle and shuffle the contents and then add boiled rice, soya sauce. Ajeenvemoto, salt and black pepper and mix all the ingredients thoroughly.

Finally, mix chopped hen and pork to the above and mix fully. Serve hot.

MUGHLAI BIRYANI

INGREDIENTS

250 gms basmati rice
1/2 cup milk
2 Nos green chillies
1 Pc ginger
100 gms curd
1 TSP mint leaves
1/2 TSP cumin
Salt to taste

75 gms onion
2 Nos red chillies
1 Pc lemon
250 gms mutton
50 gms almond (kernel)
2 Nos potato
Green corriander leaves

PROCESS

Clean rice and soak in water. Clean meat and wash-with water. Grind 1/2 quantity of onion, corriander, mint, garlic, ginger, red and green chillies. Mix curd with these ingredients and also add pieces of meat and let the contents remain mixed for an hour or so. Warm ghee in the cooker and fry balance quantity in the ghee. Remove fried onion from cooker. Put in meat, (seasoned with curd and spieces,) Cookes and fry. Add 1/2 glassfull of water to it and cover with cooker's top (lid) and let it cook for 10-12 minutes. Now remove meat from out of the cooker, and put in rice and 4 cups of water therein and cook uptil firsh whistle sounds. Remove rice from the cooker. Put ghee in the cooker and crockle the cardamon seeds, and carefully mix almonds, salt and spices with rice. Extract and add juice of one lemon alongwith saffron dissolved in milk.

To begin with spread a layer of rice in a separate pan, the spread layer of meat over rice, so on and so forth. Spread onion's round pieces upon each layer. Your Mughlai Biryani is ready.

JAPANI CHICKEN

INGREDIENTS

 1 Pc coere or lien
 100 gms ghee
 1 TSP black pepper
 2 TSP garam masala
 50 gms rice
 50 gms onion
 1 TSP vinegar
 Salt to taste

PROCESS

Clean cour/heat thoroughly. First of all fry all the spices in warm ghee in a pan and then roast/ fry cook. When it fries, then put in water (1st above cock's flesh level) and let it cook.

Grind rice to fine form on a pastel and put in the pan when cock is half-baked. When gravy becomes thicker, add vinegar and remove from fire.

MIXED BIRIYANI

INGREDIENTS

2 cups boiled rice

250 gms chicken (chopped)

1 Pc carrot

2 Pcs green onion

1/2 TSP red chillies

Salt to taste

Oil

2 Eggs

250 gms finely chopped hain

4 Pcs mushroom

1 Pc capsicum

1/2 TSP turmeric

PROCESS

Heaten a TSP of oil, add a pinch of chillies and fry shuffled eggs in the oil and keep it apart.

Fry hain in 2 TSP oil. Fry green onion, capsicum, carrot, mushroom salt, turmeric and rice chillies in balance quantity of oil. When these ingredients fully fry add eggs, chicken and hain. Add requisite quantity of water and let all the contents cook.

When all the ingredients get fully cooked, mix boiled rice and serve hot.

GOANI BROTH/ SOUP

INGREDIENTS FOR RICE

2 TSP rice
1 TBSP cream
2 Nos cloves

2 Pcs onion
Salt to taste
2 TBSP ghee

INGREDIENTS TO PROCESS PASTE

1/2 grated coconut
4 cloves of garlic
1 TSP oil
1/2 TSP cumin
1 TSP poppy seeds

1 TBSP corriander seeds
  (whole)
1 Pc chopped onion
8 Nos capsicum
Salt to taste

INGREDIENTS TO PROCESS SOUP

3 cups assorted boiled
    vegetables
50 gms cashew nut (fried)
1/2 TSP cheese
Salt to taste

1 TBSP cream
2 TBSP ghee
2 Pcs tomato
2 onions (fried)
Sugar

PROCESS

To begin with grate coconut and extract its juice (milk). Fry onion and cloves in ghee. Then add rice, salt and milk of coconut and cook. Prepare suitable paste from all the ingredients meant for preparing paste by mixing some water grate tomatoes. Fry in ghee all the spices and add grated tomatoes, boiled vegetables and cook. In necessary, add some water to it. When the contents cook fully, add cream sugar and salt.

Before serving spread soup in a baking tray and spread rice thereupon. Garnish with fried onion and cashew nut and cover.

Let the contents bake for 20 minutes in an oven serve hot.

IV. OUR DIET

We can now easily conclude as to how easy it is to process various rice delicacies with the help of guidelines, details and methods presented in this book. Hereinafter, details and relevant tabulations will be give to drive home the point as to how and in what way various food items help to generate energy(calories) in our body in order to assist us in maintaining ideal health.

NUTRIENTS

The food items which we consume, have the following mutrients :

1. Protien
2. Vitamins (A, B, C and D)
3. Fats
4. Carbohydrates (Sugars and cercals)
5. Minerals (Iron, salt and calcium etd.)
6. Water

All the said nutrients are inherent in various food items that we normally consume. It raw food items are exceedingly washed (than is actually required), the food values are drained out and get depicted. Do not peel skin thickly of any vegetable nor soak/ wash them for longer duration in water as vegetables help to fortify and strengthen our teeth and bones. Cereals, sweet potato, potatoes and fats etc provide energy to our body. Milk and milk products hold an important role in the development of our body.

Whatever eat should be masticated thoroughly so that the same readers our in a liquefied form there is body's acceptance also otherwise our intestines have to overfirection in order to digest food, resulting in midigestion, our food should be such as could be easily digested so that aids in proper growth and development of all organs of our body.

VARIOUS SOURCES TO OBTAIN NUTRIENTS FROM FOOD

Let us now consider the food items that can prove as sources of various nutrients and also that which of such nutrients can nurture our body. We should also know the fall out conpact of shuch nutrients which remain on deficient supply.

1. POTIEN

Sources: Milk and milk products, meats, fish, pulses, eggs are known sources of proteins.

Benefits: Help in growth and development of body, fibres, and also rebuild fibres. If protiens remains in constant supply to our body in old age, it keeps our body in a healthy state other wise many protien deficiency result in multiple disorders and deformities

Disadvantages: Depleted shortage of protien supply in habits or restricts formation of fibres due to which body's development comes to a stand still, height of body cannot pick up and body remains diseased and along with poor health.

VITAMINS:—
VITAMIN 'A'

Sources: Milk green vegetables, eggs, papaya, carrot etc. are usual sources of vitamin 'A'

Benefits: It keeps our eyes healthy and one may not require spects even at an elderly age. Helps to read without glasses. Keeps up glaze and tenderness (softness of body, helps to develop body.

Disadvantages: Vitamin 'A' deficiency causes weakness if vision and might telendness. Then becomes dry, nose and throat also get infected.

VITAMIN 'B'

Sources: Milk, cheese, curd, why and other milk products, cereals, eggs green and leafy vegetables, dry fruits, (like cashew nut, almond, vaisuis, peanut, pure nut, dry apricot, ground not kernet etc.)

Advantages: Digestion system function abby and normally. There is far less apprehension and chances of heart diseases. Nerves get sugar and flexible rather entire nervous system stays healthy and functional.

Disadvantages: Vitamin-B deficiency results in depraved and weak digestion, as food is digested quite take entire digestive apparantus gets weakened and inperative, there is loss of appetite (Amorexia), face is dry and luster less, there is fungus growth in the ears lips crack, there are thences of Bery-Bery diseases.

VITAMIN 'C'

Sources: Green and leafy vegetables myrobialon (Amlake or Amla), sprouled pulses/grains, tomato, lemon, orange, guava, mango, rasberry etc. are the sources of vitamin 'C'. In fact, all citrus fruits contain plenty of vitamin 'C' in them.

Advantages: It strengthens teeth, doesn't let infection inflict the gums, helps in quicker and early healing of wounds, raises resistance of the body to ward off chances of infection.

Disadvantages 'C': Vitamin deficiency results weak, unhealthy teeth and geims. Growth gets retarcted. Due to work gains teeth cannot could themselves in the socket, there is llteeding from genus due to their being spongy.

VITAMIN 'D'

Sources: The cheaptest and most easily available source for this vitamin is sunrays. It can also be obtained from milk and milk products, eggs (yellow portion), liver fish oil etc.

Advantages: Helps to strenghten bones keep teeth in healthy condition (its deficiency can cause rickets in infants/ children). It helps body to properly absorb calcium in women.

FATS

Sources: Ghee, oil, butter, dry fruits

Advantages: Provide heat and strength to body.

Disadvantages: Excess of fats causes clearrlioes/motions excessive glaziness of skin, arterio/ allero sckerosis, heart ailments, dyspion, laugh blood pressure, obesity, pains in joints, bones and muscles etc.

CABOSE OR CARBOHYDRATES

Sources: grain careals, pulses, sugars, (ladose, frutose and surcose) beetroot, potato, sugar cane etc.

Advantages: Carbohydrates are an essential sources of energy and heat and do not let over body weaken.

Disadvantages: Body gets tired again and again, even on minimal exertion, weakness increases due to which our body weakens and emaciates. There is also risk of lack of sugar in blood.

MINERALS AND SALTS

Calcium

Sources: Curd, calcium, apple, lime, milk etc.

Advantage: It assists in proper growth of teeth, makes our bones stronger, helps in bony development and growth of a cluld.

Disadvantages: Teeth weaken, crimble and breath, bones become fragile and powerless, blood clothing process felts delayed. Its deficiency also results in anemia.

IRON

Sources: Jaggery, dates, bananas, onion, spinach

Advantages: Iron helps to maintain and enhance haemoglobin in the blood. It is a career of oxygen.

Disadvantages: Deficiency of iron results in poor quality and quantity of blood, anaric conditions, loss of strength and resistance of our body.

WATER

Sources: All drinks, particularly milk, tea, aereted and soft drinks, whey, sugar cane juices, juices of fruits and vegetables, other liquids. But plain water is, by far, the the cheapest and best.

Advantages: water helps to maintain restore boiled circulation in the body, seirets toxens from the body, removes faecal matter and urine, excretes sweat, keeps proper balance in the body.

Disadvantages: Blood flow and blood circulation are adversely affected, digestive system gets erratic due to which there is an ongoing complaint of constipated bowels. Body temperature remains high due to lack of water intake.

PRINCIPLE GROUPS OF FOOD-ITEMS

Above description of various nutrients gives a bird's eye view of the advantages disadvantages and sources of food items, for the canvemence of the readers. We are spelling out various groups of food items which should be utilised in our daily diet's proform as a matter of routine so that our body stays healthy and fit.

MILK AND MILK PRODUCTS

• Milk and its various products (not ghee or butter) are the main in gredients/sources for protein, vitamins and salts. Main function of this food group is the develop the body and repair our weak and or damaged fibers.

• <u>Animal food products and Pulses:</u> Meat, fish, eggs and pulses are the main sources of protein, salt and vitamins. They help in repairing our damaged body fibers and restore and cultivate energy.

• <u>Fruits and vegetables:</u> We also obtain vitamins and salts from this group. These food items keep our body in a healthy state and also build up general resistance of the body so as to fight against infections, diseases and in vading foreign elements.

CO-EATS

They are the main source of energy which, helps to provide strength, power and energy to our body.

MEAL TIMINGS

Generally our routine dietary programme consists of —
1. Morning Breakfast
2. Lunch (mid-day meals)
3. Evening tea (breakfast in the evenings)

4. Dinner

Intake of food will depend on health or diseased condition of the body but following guidelines are general paranthes/standards for a normal and healthy person which any healthy and normal person can adhere to.

BREAKFAST

A cup of tea or coffee is quite useful easily in the morning. After attending to routine calls of nature, one can take Parantha, bread slieces, dosa or idly. If you do not wish to exert, bread shlies and butter combination is the best combination. In addition you can have milk, tea or coffee alongside.

LUNCH

Avoid heavy and heavy fried delicacies, as this is the mefor meals' time. Rotis or chapatis processed out of wheat flour (which should be light) or rice. Add sufficient quantity of cooked vegetables and pulses. But cooked vegetables should not be heavily fired or should they cause any monotony or revulsion. Food must be to one's taste, you should also add raita, curd, why salads, etc. make your lunch suitable healthy and tasty. Salad should be prepared according to food items available in a particular season, for which tomato celery onion, radish, carrot, lemon, leaves of green vegetables, mint and /or corriander leaves may be used.

DINNER

Dinner should light, nutritions and suitable. After dinner one generally retires to bed. Hence eat only those food items which can be digested easily chapatis and rice form an essential part of our dinner's manner. You can take pulses, dry or juicy vegetables but use only minival quantity of ghee, oil or spices. Take also light salads at night with your meals in addition to curd or raita.

To make your lunch and dinner meals more tasty and deleitable you can use pickles, sauce, jains or soup which also assist in quicker digestion of meals. If you ever feel monotonous or bored, you can use 'Purees' occasionally.

Sweet dish or dessert should be a part of your diet, as it saliates your taste buds. If you wish to maintain good health, you take a glassfull of water, prior to going to your bed.

EVENING TEA

You can take some light breakfast in the evening, like saltish/sweat biscuits, fried dals moth with tea or coffee. Ton can replace tea and coffee with juices of frouits.

In summer season, cold milk, jaljeera, lemon sugar juice, whey etc. will stand you in good stead.

V. BALANCED AND NUTRITIVE DIET

Everyone takes his diet but the chief consideration is whether the same is digested by the body. There is a direct relation between diet and its assimilation (digestion) and, unless both the facets remain properly and suitably balanced, one cannot derive requisite & desirable benefits. A balanced and nutritive diet is that which consiste of carbohydrates, protien, fats vitamins, minerals, green and leafy vegetables and milk and its products, that is our body must be fed with due and requisite quantity of each essential nutrient. For a balanced and nutritive diet, all the necessary food stems should be included in daily diet.

Diet which we take normally should be taken after taking into consideration over age, sex, body's requirements, health status, height, type and load of professional foli etc. Our body is ordained in such a meticulous way that it sends natural warning signal's when it is not supplied with reqiuisite quantity of any essential nutrient. It is another matter whether take note and cognizance of such warning signals. No disease surfaces suddenly rather the same developes in phases. If you ever suffer from flatulance, acidity, adidic/ citure eructations gurgling of flatus etc. you must get warned that some indiscretion and relaxation, regarding food intake, has been committed. Ingrance or neglect of such symptoms can laved you in more complicated position.

If you apply your mind and properly analyse the kind and quantity of any food item that has either been a new addition to your dietary milk or if your have taken any item excess of the normal intake, you will immediately be able to discern and locate the food item which has disturbed your metabolic process. That is some excessive, indiscreet and undesirable food item's intake is the culprit which has brought about the present distressed and agonzing situation. To offset ill effects of such undesirable food items, it is better to eliminate the same from your diet.

Remember, you are the best judge of your body and its chemistry and you know fully well what suits you or not. Even your own family doctor cannot pinpointedly tell the disturbing factors which have wrought present predicament. If you tell your doctor about the food intake and the food items honestly, it is only then that your doctor can treat you. Hence adjure such food items that do not fit in your slot. Prevention of contributory cause is the only way to solve your problems. Try to lcate the cousative factor, try to avoid the disturbing and harmful food items, try to take note of nature's initial warnings signal and finally take corrective measures — this way you can easily discern, dispel and correct the imbalances.

Following tables will clearly guide you, regarding intake of essential nutrients. Let it be remembered that every person needs food to sustain and nurture the body but, then, which foods will meet the required demands on energy intake and expanse, will depend upon the nature of an individual's nature of job.

Calorie is an energy measuring unit. Number of calories required will be determined by factors like age, sex, nature of jole, health status etc. For instance a person working in an office (sitting jole) will require far less calories than wood-cutter, manual labour, athlete and sports person. A pregnant lady, an elderly person, and infant and a child, a young person in growth stage, a bed-ridden patient in hospital or at home, will require different amount of energy. The criterion is between generation and expension of energy. Hence there must a proper balance between generated energy and expense. If there is imbalance between the two facts, ill health is the only out come. For instance, if your body generates more energy but there is total absence in lack of physical activity, one will put on weight and resultant healty hazards. Conversely, if one performs strenous work, but doesn't feed or compensate his body with requisite calories, he will feel run down, amaciated and weak. Most of the physical disorders emanate due to imbalance between energy generation and expense thereof. If you wish to stay free from diseases, you must work out a proper balance between calorie generation and its expense by physical activity.

When we discuss total nutrition, we cannot and must not ignore our body's food requirements which ought to be matched with proper physical activity. A dietician can better advise you about your diet, keeping in view all the fallors stated earlier. No doubt parameters and criterea go on changing every-now-and then, and this is an ongoing process. But each person's food requirements vary, due to the factors enumerated earlier.

Comparative table may be studied. The information dissanated is merely a guidling and is not the last word on calorie and food intake. At least, it will provide for an initial launching pad to begin with.

VI. SOME DIETARY RULES

• Eat only when you are hungry. It is a bad habit to go on churning every-now-and then. Untimely food intake is infurious for health. If previously taken food has not been digested properly and system is again overloaded with extra food, it will disturb metablic process due to undigested food, as digestive juices will not mix with food which will result in dypepsia, indigestion, constipation, or loose motions, flatinlence, abdominal colic, gas runbling in abdome, sour/acdic erectations etc.

• Food must be taken at a desigested lame daily. If however, you happen to miss your meal-time, it is better to stop over of forego your food than to ingest at a wrong time and unnecessarily overload your stomach.

• Eat only when you really fed the meal to eat often your system will send your signals, demanding from you to take your meals — this is called 'Jatharagani' in Ayurveda. If you feel to take not of your body's demand for food or foil to satiate your appetite, or if your fail to delay the process of food intake, body's demand for food will dimnish, resulting in flatulance, slothness, pain in abdomen, loose motions etc.

• If you fail to satiat your body's urge/demand for food , or ignore it, you will face health hazards in the form of evaliation, reluctance to engage yourself in work, a feeling of fatigue and inactivity or indolence.

• If our body is like a machine and each machine requires energy to operate it. If energy is not supplied, the machine cannot function, similarly if body is not compensated / supplied with the requisite amount of energy, all the physical activities will come to a stands till resulting in an all round low level of activity and functioning of our body. Food intake is not a compulsion, it is the basic necessity of body. If daily routine is chalked out and planned in a maticulous and time-bound frame, there is no reason why food cannot be taken at the designated/fixed time. Regularity and punctuality in food timings is prerequisite or better health and life.

• Ayurveda has chalked out certain conditions regarding food intake — one should take meals only after defecating and passing urine when mind is peaceful, five elements are well balanced, there is no wind in the stomach, body is light, all the congentive and intake clual faculties, senses are functioning normally, there is appetite.

• It is harmful and wrong to go on eating in-between two principle meals (lunch and dinner). Also do not eat or drink anything uptil an hour after taking exercise. Further there must be a gap of 2 hours between food intake and sex act.

• To free the body from toxins, excreta etc. the ideal time is said to be between 4 am and 12 noon. During this period ingest only very light food which should simply help to sustain and maintain strength and resistance of the body.

• There should be a gap of 12 hours between morning breakfast and dinner timings.

• Take only light and easily digestible food at might due to the fail that there is no physical activity during night.

• Have a scroll after dinner so that food taken gets digested.

• Nothing should be eaten from the inception to concluding period of fast. You will fail to derive any advantage by keeping yourself on fast, if you eat specy, heavily fried, conducted and rich food. If you do so, your object and desired advantages of keeping on farst will suffer a setback. Mian purpose behind fast is to correct and rectify ill effects of wrong and excessive eating, provide rest to the body, but it is never intended to make up for the deficiency of food, by over-loading your system with undesirable, harmful and damaging food items.

• Your food should necessarily be balanced, nutri tive, timely, regular, easily digestible pure and simple. Remember, we eat to live and not that we live to eat by which tern it implies that food is a means to sustain our body but is not end in itself.

• Keep your digestive capacity in mind, while. Consuming meals and also take your meals at a regular time daily.

REASONS FOR TAKING MEALS AT A DESIGNATED TIME

When digestive juices are released by our stomach, it helps to digest food quickly and the body again gets ready for ingestion of more food. Mouth is the only organ for food-intake, though in diseased state food may have to be given via nosal passages or rective. All the body organs function due to the mouth remaining opened, as food can gain entry into stomach via-mouth's passage only. When food gets properly digested eructations generate and wind also passes out outomatically, without any hassles, and there is no foul odour either. In addition, all the digestive juices continue to be generated by body in a regular and time-bound manner. If stool, urine & wind get expelled systematically and regularly, there is no undue strain on heart.

HOW TO EAT

Body can derive optimum milkage from food if the same is eaten in proper way, under noted points, if kept in mind, will help in working a scheduled daily routine, at least as far as food intake is concerned.

• Wash your hands, face, feet and mouth thoroughly and properly and splash cold water over the eyes as, by doing so, you will feel free of fatigue, your body will be felt to be fresh and light.

• If possible, squat on the floor and then take your meals. It will help in proper and digestion of the ingested food.

• It may sound a bit innocuous and strange that, a person who eats only once is an ascetic (Yogi), one who eats twice is a family person (Bhogi) and who eats thrice is an ailing person (Rogi) but this is a time-tested and factual maxin.

• Do not gulp food down your gullet, rather masticate the same thoroughly. If food is eaten quickly and hastily and without being masticated, the food fails to segregate into fine particles. When such broken and undigested food reaches our stomach, the stomach has to exert hard. Teeth are meant for mastication and if food is not masticated properly, the stomach has to put in extra effort and intestines compensate for the undone foli of teeth. This process turns turtle entire digestive system.

• Every one of us knows fully well that if food is thoroughly masticated through teeth, saliva will get mixed with our food. Not only that, but gradual mastication breaks our food into fine particles and also strengthens and exercises our teeth. Through sustained and gradual mastication, saliva contencies to mix with food, and thus food gets broken into fine particles and it gets liquified. When liguified food readers our intestines, digestive enzymes and juice mix with it easily and, by this process, no undue pressure is exerted on the stomach and intestines, and food gets digested quickly and easily.

• Never take your meals if and when you are in a hurry, there is tension in the mind, mind is at inrest, you are riddled and burdened with some problem, are angry and agitated. If you are ever confronted with such problems and, even then, opt to take your meals, you will simply harm yourself, as food will turn into poison (not literally). Whenever your mind and body are under any type of stress and strain, entire body chemistry changes for the worse due to adverse impacts cast on our endocrine glands, resulting in diminished/excessive release of glandular secretions. Such changes cast adverse impart upon our entire nerves system, so much so that nerves get agitated and tense. Hence, take your meals only when you are fully satisfied, peaceful, tension-free, from all worries, enxieties and cares and in a fit frame of mind and carefree. Never take your meals hastily.

WHAT TO AVOID IN FOOD

• Your food ought to be pure, clean and fresh but not state, putred, delayed or overcooked.

• Highly spiced, fried, condimented, heavy, where too must of spices, oil or ghee has been used, must be avoided as it exerts undue stress and strain on the digestive system. Such a type of food will pave the way for obesity, indigestion flatulence, gas and other digestion related disorders.

• Do not consume water immediately, midway of after taking meals. If your opt to do so, digestive juices and enzymes will take much longer time to intermingle with food particles, resulting in delayed digestion, inaddition to body being deprevied of advantages of essential nutrients. Hence, take water an hour after finishing your meals.

• Avoid using juices of fruits, vegetables, immediately, before, during or after meals, as fruit juices get digested much earlier as compared to vegetable juices which take comparatively much longer time to get digested.

• Do not mix up fruit and vegetable juices, due to the factors enumerated above. If, at all, it is necessary to take juice the same should be taken an hour prior to taking your meals. Do not consume any liquid or fried food item with your diet. In short, do not use any liquid product, including water immediately before, during or after taking your meals.

• Your food must include all the essential nutrients. If food is nutretively dificient, the body will not be able to dirive full advantage from food, resulting in change in physical chemistry, weakness of body organs and nutritional deficiency related disorders.

• Try to eat only pure and simple food. Avoid using meats, fish and such food items that take longer time to get digested. Such food items adversely affect digestive process, agitate blood vessels. Meat is a food product for the animals and not for the human beings. Whenever reference is made to power, it is always turned as 'horse power', and horse is purely a vegetarian animal, though there are more powerful animals than horse. Hence try to stick to vegetarian diet which should be an inspirable entity of your daily diet as, by eating meat, only your taste buds will be satiated but not your body which will remain deprived of strength.

• Always avoid the eatables and drinks that are freely available in the market as you are not aware of the standard of hygene; cooking medium, quality of food items used and method of cooking. Do not ever eat 'Fast Foods' which is now termed as 'Junk Food' by the westerners. Fruit juice which are published as fresh fruit juices are neither fresh nor even hygienic but, despite that, people themselves consume and also serve to visitors. Artificial flavours and colours are used in 'canned' and buttled so-called 'Fruit Juices' — they cause immense and irreparable health hazards. Hence always avoid them. Even so called fresh cane juice is neither fresh nor hygienic and can cause loose motions, vomiting, nausea etc. Avoid also canned and boiled soft drinks.

• Fruit-chat, dahi-vada, chowmeen, chana-kulcha or Bhatura, exposed kulfi, cut and exposed fruits, pakauras etc., as they are capable of cause untold health problems. Hence, if you avoid eating such harmful delicacies, you will not only safeguard your health but also save your hard earned money. If, at all, you cannot resist the temptation of consuming the said food preparations, those should better be processed at home. Food items prepared at home are cheaper, safer for health and highly pure, hygenic and trustworthy. Above all, you will have satisfaction that the food you have consumed is free from infection. Commercial sale outlets have no concern for your health, they are simply aiming upon your pocket. In fact, you not only shell out money but also invite health hazards.

• Food taken must can form to one's need, place, temperament physical condition, body chemistry and nature. Regional foods are ordained and processed in such a way and with only those ingredients which suit the climatic conditions prevailing in a specific zone or area and that's the sole reason as to why there is a radical difference in northern, southern, western and eastern areas' foods which meet requirements and demands of climatic conditions exerting in a zone / area.

• Do not consume foods that do not suit you or are known causes of causing certain reactions, ailments and upsets and also avoid food items which your doctor has directed you not to use. Moreover, if you adopt regional food habits, there are far less chances of your contracting any disease as mother niture, in her wisdom, grows only those vegetations which are necessary for the habitants of a particular area. But, all the same, you must use your disecretion in choosing the foods, out of the available stock, that suit you best. Do not be guided or tempted by the advice and eulogisation, about certain foods and food items, which are known to cause you health problems. Hence be your own judge.

• Untimely, half-cooked or under/over cooked, unhygienic, stale and rotten foods must be given a go-bye. Wrong and harmful foods will spoil your health and of none else. Hence always be contious in selecting your food items. Food is meant to impart energy, strength and resistance to you and any food item that fails to meet such requirements, deserves to be discarded outright.

• Water-horse diseases are many and rempant, hence always drink pure and clean water which is free from sediments, becteria and other impurities. Water purifying Gadgets, availabe in the market, carry only cosmetic utility and do not give any tangible benefits. If water is impure, dirty, replete with becteria, the best and cheapest way is to boil the, let it cool, and then consume the same.

VII.
PRECAUTIONS NEEDED ON SEASON-BASED FOOD ITEMS' SELECTION AND USE

GENERAL INFORMATION

An year has three main seasons, viz. Summer, cold, and rainy and in each season all the vegetations do not grow uniformly. The vegetations, that grow in a particular season only those should be used. It is repeated that while deciding to opt for any food item, you must take into account your nature, body requirement, health status, climate, place/region etc.

As far as possible try to take only balanced and nutritive diet which is replete with essential nutrients, like corbody drates, protiens, fats, minerals, vitamins, milk and milk products, seasonal green and leafy vegetables and fruits, pulses etc.

It is an unfounded notion, rather a myth, to believe that costly food items help to maintain an ideal health, nor is it also true that high speed fired, heavily condimented food items are sources of energy and strength to the body. It is a common knowledge that soyabean contains much more protien than fish, carrots can able replace apples, spinach for costly haematinic tonics, milk for calcium etc.

It is unwise and indiscreet to squander money on costly and non-seasoned food items, as you can easily substitute them with cost effective and equally beneficial food items that are easily and freely available. Do not run after social status which carries only a cosmetic value. Elite class takes pleasure in consuming costly food-items in off-season. This only a cheap type of self pride and status. Hence be a realistic and not imaginative and unpractical.

In our country summer is the longest season, followed closely by winter and rainy seasons, the order descending. But due to pollution and other such factors ecological balance has been enormously disturbed. Process of seasonal changes has turned turtle the sequence and duration of each season, as there is summer when it should been cold, and vice verse, and when there should be rains, it is a period of humidity/ draught. Off seasons rains has become common phenomenon. Entire sequence and order of season has got disturbed and gone haywire. Hence, it has now become difficult to adjust one's diet as per natural conditions. If there is no heat, snow won't melt on the monutains and when snow doesn't melt, the river will have depleted water. Extension or reduction of any season, beyond its normal duration, is a red signal for the people.

No doubt, it takes plenty of time to change one's food habits to new pattern or in accordance with local conditions and resultant demands of seasons. But sustained effort will facilitate change-over to new food pattern, but put utmost patience is called for the achieve this end. As a person's habits die hard so also his food habits much longer time to change. You shouldn't expect miracle overnight as you must give requisite and proper time to your body to adjust itself to the changed place, climate and environs. Hence, sustained, persistent and patient endeavour is required to effect changes in habits and, more so, in food habits. If you act otherwise, your mind and body will revolt against your efforts; hence be patient and preservance.

The guidelines, pertaining to use of certain food items, are general and not specific. You can easily adapt the tendered suggestions to your own requirements.

FOOD DURING WINTER SEASON
EDIBLE FOOD ITEMS DURING WINTER SEASON

Due to impact of cold the body loses its warmth, hence body needs to be kept warmed, either by proper clothing or food items or both. Main food items that impart heat to the body are garlic, ginger, green gram (moong) ghee, milk and its products, jaggery, wheat, dry fruits, corriander, dry ginger. Fencegreen, loddoos of corriander seeds, laddoos of basan (gram flour), coconut, cloves apple, grapes, mlta, orange, cherry, meats, chicken, fish, eggs, oils etc.

PROHIBITED FOOD ITEMS

Always try to avoid cold beverages or drinks, cold food, edible items that are capable of causing wind/gers. Also do not consume much heavy and fried food, bitter, pungent, urad etc. Do not use ice in any form.

SPECIAL REMARKS

Consume only easily digestible and heat generating food items. Whatever is eaten in the winter gets easily digested as heat in the body exists in sufficient quantity to help in digestion of food. In addition, keep your body fully clad with warm clothings so as to rule out any danger of exposure to cold, cold winds dry winds or snowy winds. Proper and sufficient food is complementary to each other. Some people are intrinsically allergic to some dry fruits, fruits and vegetables etc. hence do not adopt a lopsided approach.

FOOD DURING SUMMER SEASON

During hot season there is too much and an almost continuous thirst, as water gets exerted through heet of sun, persperation, urination etc. If loose motions take place, even the residual content in the body is lost and urinary flow is also scant. If dehydration sets in life can be in danger, as there is also depletion or total loss of salts from the body. Hence water-sodium balanced. Must be maintained in the body. Consume planty of sugar and salt mixed water to compensate for loss of water and sodium. In order to pre-empt danger of loose motions, dehydration, excessive thirst take plenty of liquids in the form of juice of fruits, lemon. Mousambi, orange, coconut, barley water, syrup of rose, poppy seeds, phalsa, bitter gourd, mint, onion, gourd, vinegar, cane juice, corriander (green leaves). Liquified milk and curd, watermelon, muskmelon, turmeric, cucumber, pomegranate whey etc. Whenever there is need to move out take plenty of water, adding some table salt also and continue to replenish water content. Take plenty of juicy vegetables, juices etc.

PROHIBITED FOOD ITEMS

Avoid taking hot meals, take food when it is cold. Do not use species, ghee, butter, vegetable oils, liquour, tobacco/ smoking, dry food items and also those food items that precipitate and cause thurst tea, coffee, cocoa, meats, fish, fish oil, eggs, dry fruits etc. Do not move put when hot winds/too below and protect your body from adverse effects of heat and heat stroke. Do not wear too tight clothes. If possible use a solar hot or wrap small tower or large sized hanky around back side of neck or wear a cap or turban or use an umbrella. When you are back, do not take cold water, rather rise your mouth with water.

SPECIAL DIRECTIONS

Heat stroke or loo affects only when there is no water in the body; hence take plenty of water before morning out. You can take water, quite often, even while you are mobile. Water drunk from an earthen pitcher quenches thirst and prevents repeated desire to drink water, whereas iced water does provide some relief initially but causes thirst more rapidly. Syrup of barley power (sattoo) keeps body cool and doesn't cause thirst, in addition it is a diuretic also. If neat, clean, pure and freshly extracted sugar cane juice is taken, it will dispel heat and thirst. It is also diureitc but excessive intake can cause loose motions.

Roast raw (green) mangoes and extract juice therefrom, add salt, water, sugar or jaggery — it is an excellent preventor of heat and heat stroke. Tamarind should be soaked in water and juice extracted, adding some salt, sugar and black pepper also. Lemon juice, with salt and sugar, also prevents one from gravity and ill effects of heat.

Lastly as cases of diarrhoea, cholera, vomiting and nausea are quite common in summer season, it is dangerous to eat, drink anything outside your home; so as to rule out chances of infection and heat.

At digestive power weakens during this season, there is also loss weight and appetite, hence one should lay more stress on liquids.

FOOD DURING RAINY SEASON

During rainy days body becomes sloth and indolent, digestion gets weak, there is disinclination for doing any work, inclination to sleep, there is also some amount of drawsiness, tiredness, physical activity is hampered, also there is absence of alacrity, cough and wind increase, skin diseases surface, diarrhoea or dysentry, pain in body, vomiting, nausea and imbalance amongst three humors (viz wind, bile and phlegm) creates vitiatio, resistance power weakens. Untimely and incalled for food intake further precipitates the aforesaid unfavourable states.

Take only light and easily digestable diet, in the form of khichri, Moong, spicy and cooked vegetables, old rice, tea, coffee etc. Use also butter eatables and drinks (not liquir) (like bitter gourd and margosa), Battua, ginger, garlic, mint, corriander, onion etc. Keep high standard of personal hygiene and thoroughly wash under arm portion, thigh folds, private parts, ears, neck etc. After taking bath, completely dry up your body as moisture can cause foul small, bad sweat, various skin disorders etc. Do not let your body drench with rain water as you can easily be subjected. To bad cold, coryza, nasal discharge, cough, congestion in chest, dysurea or else polyurea, feverishness, pain and ache in body etc. Constipation is a common complaint during rainy season which can be cured by taking 1 TSP of triphela at night with hot water. If you suffer from loose motions take coconut water beal fruit, khichri, moong etc. But, in any case, do not be complacent and indiscreet in using your food options. Here reasonable precuation is the only watchword. Partial fasting can be useful to avert chances of physical problems.

PROHIBITED FOOD ITEMS AND PRECUATIONS

Impure water is the chief culprit in causing diseases during rainy season. Hence, never take raw water. Mix a tablet of chlorine to 20 litres of water or boil water to boiling point, let it cool and then use the same. Wash all raw fruits and vegetables with fresh water. Do not consume pakauras, chat pakauri, fast food, stale and putrid items, exposed fruit (cut) pieces, sugarcane juice, juice of fruits and vegetables, Dahi-bara, fruit-chat, cold drinks, ice-cream etc.

Eat less than your body's demand. Do not use lassi, cold, raw milk, meat, fish etc. Resort may be health hot beverages like tea, coffee, cocoa or herbal tea or lime tea with honey. Also avoid using vegetable oils, ghee, butter and various other types of fat.

Take a tablet of vitamin-C (500 mg) daily to sustain your resistance power. For cough relates problems use dry ginger, honey, black pepper, black salt, cumin, cardamom, cinnamon etc., provide you are not allergic to them.

Immediately remove your drenched clothes, dry up your body wear dry clothes, Restain your extremist tendencies. Sunrays are quite sharp during rainy season which can scorch your tender stage and render your skin darken. Hence use an umbrella. Apply Lacto Calamine lotion to your move sensitive body parts before you move oil in the sun.

VIII.

Miscellaneous information regarding calories, activity related calorie expense, age-related calorie requirement and nutrietional values of various food items.

CALORIE

The energy that we derive from diet/food is measured and nomenclated as 'Calorie' which, in fact, is an energy measuring unit and the calories (energy), expended during physical exertion, is called calorie burnt (during the course of physical exercise and exertion). Number of calories required by a person is dependent on the nature of job and the calories burnt/expended, amount of labour put in to discharge his work, age, sex, climate. A child, during the growth stage and also during playing games, an old person leading a sedentary life style, a person working in an office, a manual balourer, a stone-cutter, tree-feller, a pregnant woman, during and after pregnancy, a hospitalised patient will require different percentage of calories. Simple rule is; the more energy one spends the higher calories he would require. When we talk of calories, total calories required by a person during duration of 24 hours, will be reckoned by total calories obtained from various sources of nutrition. Two persons of the same height, age and same work-load would require, different amount of calories because metabolism of each person differs. Every one is a law unto himself, when above criteria are taken into consideration. Two main groups, viz of vegetarians and non-vegetarians, have to work out food items which, when combined, give total calories required by a person. There is another class which adheres to both the said types of food categories.

As already indicated, a balanced diet must be a unified entity, consisting of cereals, gree vegetables, fibre, fruits, milk and its various products, meats etc. so that the dietary intake presents a homogenous combination of essential carbohydrates, proteins, fats, minerals, vitamins etc. It is a myth that costly foods give better nutrietious values than the cheaper ones but, luckily, the fact is the other way round. So, when working out your food and diet, you should be more conscious of the nutritional factor than the cost factor. Main purpose is, and should be, to meet calorie requirement of the body than the money spent therefor.

In the following table an effort has been made to spell out calories spent by an individual, in relation to his physical activity (For all sexes, age-groups)

ACTIVITY RELATED CALORIE EXPENSION

Activity	*Calories expended per hour*
(i) Light Activity	**50-200 Calories' group**
Lying down/sleeping	80
Sitting	100
Driving a car	120
House-hold work	180
(ii) Moderate Activity	**200-300 Calories' group**
Bicycling (8.25 kms)	210
Walking (4.25 kms)	210
Gardening	220
Canoeing (4.25 kms)	230
Golf	250
Lawn-moving (Power mover)	250
Lawn-mowing (Hand mover)	270
Bowling	270

(iii)	**Marked Activity**	**300-400 Calories' Group**
	Walking (6 kms)	300
	Swimming (40 Mtrs.)	300
	Rowing (4.25 kms)	300
	Fencing	300
	Badminton	350
	Horse-Riding (Trotting)	350
	Roller-Skating	350
	Volley Ball	350
	Square Dancing	350
	Table — Tennis	360
(iv)	**Vigorous Activity**	**Over 400 Calories' Group**
	Ice — skating (16 kms)	400
	Sawing or wood-chopping	400
	Tennis	420
	Hill-climbing	480
	Skiing	490
	Hand ball	600
	Bicycling (21 kms)	660
	Running (16 kms)	900

DAILY CALORIE REQUIREMENTS (DURING 24 HOURS)

Age Group	Calorie Requirements
Upto 6 months	120 Calories Per kg body weight
7-12 months	100 Calories Per kg body weight
1-3 years	1200 Calories
4-6 years	1500 Calories
7-9 years	1800 Calories
10-12 years	2100 Calories
13-12 years (boys)	2500 Calories
13-15 years (girls)	2200 Calories

16-18 years (boys)	3000 Calories
16-18 years (girls)	2200 Calories
Men, Doing Light Work	2200 Calories
Men, Doing Medium Work	2800 Calories
Men, Doing Heavy Work	3400 Calories
Women, Doing Light Work	1900 Calories
Women, Doing Medium Work	2200 Calories
Women, Doing Heavy Work	2800 Calories

Note: Parameters, shown above, are merely indicative of general standards but calories for each person are required to be worked out on the basis of age, sex, amount of manual labour put in, health status, person's, height, weight and climate of a place.

1. Lactating mothers would require 700 calories extra, as long as they continue to nurse their babies.
2. Expectant shift to mothers will requires 300 calories extra, particularly during last 3-4 months of pregnancy.
3. Roughly on kilogram weight will be added extra to the body if, during a particular period of time, 3000 extra calories are added (taken) over and above normal calorie requirement.
4. Conversely; 3500 calories taken less than one's daily requirement, over a period of time, will shed one kg of body weight.
5. Above figures indicate calorie intake for normal and healthy persons but in a diseased state, calorie intake will have to be modified depending nature, status and complexity of the disorder.
6. A retired worker, aged over 60 will require 1400 calories in a day, industrial worker (aged 35-39) 1575 calories, an army cadet (aged 19-20) 1800 and a school-boy (aged

18) would require 2000 calories per days.

7. All the calorie requirements are merely guidelines; hence by no means precise, but nearer to precision.

8. Indicated calorie intake is to be divided in diets taken during a period of 24 hours.

ACTIVITY RELATED CALORIE CONSUMPTION CHART

Activity	Calorie expended Per Hour	Activity	Calorie expended Per Hour
		Miscellaneous	
Lawn Mowing		Writing	20
(Power Hower)	250	Typing	30
Lawn Mowing		Tailoring	45
(Hand Hower)	270	Shoemaking	90
Bowling	270	Carpentry	140
Marked Activity		Stone-cutting	300
Fencing	300	Coal-mining	320
Rowing (4.25 kms)	300	Sleeping	0
Swimming (40 mtrs)	300	Sitting	15
Walking (6 kms)	300	Standing	20
Badminton	350	Dressing/Undressing	33
Horse back Riding		Walking-Moderately	
(Trotting)	350	fast	215
Square Dancing	350	Walking Downstairs	290
Volleyball	350	Walking upstairs	1000

Information, on calorie expended during a particular job, is a relative factor and may not apply to one and all informally as many factors can show change in results.

NUTRIONAL VALUES OF VARIOUS FOODS

(Values based on 100 gms of edible portion of each food item)

	1 Calorie (K. Cal)	2 Protein mg	3 Fats mg	4 Minerals mg	5 Carbo hydrate	6 Calcium mg	7 Phosphorus	8 Irion mg	9 Vitamin (A/C) (10) mg
Cereals & Pulses									
Millet	361	11.6	5.0	2.3	67.5	42	296	5.0	132
Barley	336	11.5	1.3	1.2	69.6	26	215	3.0	10
Beans	346	22.9	1.3	3.2	60.6	260	410	5.8	–
Bengal Gram	360	11.1	5.3	3.0	60.9	202	312	10.2	189
Bengal Gram Dal	1347	24.0	1.4	3.2	59.6	154	385	9.1	38
Corn/Maize	348	11.1	3.6	1.5	66.2	10	348	2.0	90
Green Gram (Mag)	334	24.0	1.3	3.5	56.7	24	326	7.3	94
Peas, Dry	374	19.7	1.1	2.2	56.5	75	298	5.1	39
Rice, Milled	345	6.8	0.5	0.6	78.2	10	160	3.1	–
Peas, unpolished	346	7.5	1.0	0.9	76.7	10	190	3.2	2
Rice Bran	393	13.5	16.2	6.6	48.4	67	1410	35.0	9
Soybean	432	43.2	19.5	4.6	20.9	240	690	11.5	426
Wheat Wole	346	11.8	1.5	1.5	71.2	41	306	4.9	64
Whole wheat–Flour	341	12.1	1.7	2.7	69.4	98	355	11.5	29
Wheat flour–Refued	348	11.0	0.9	0.6	73.9	23	121	2.5	25
Wheat Germ	397	29.2	7.4	3.5	53.3	40	84.6	6.00	–
Wheat Sprout	397	29.2	7.4	3.5	53.3	40	84.0	6.00	–

(only vitamin 'A' given in I.U. and c.m. Mgs. Like other values)

Fruits and Nuts

	Moisture	Pro-tien	Fat	Mine-rals	Fibre-hydrate	Carbo-Kal	Calorie	Calcium	Phos phorous	Iron	Vitamin (A/C)
Almonds	5.2	20.8	58.9	2.9	1.7	10.5	655	230	490	4.5	0
Amla	81.8	0.5	0.1	0.5	3.4	13.7	58	50	20	1.2	Vit/C–6a
Apple	84.6	0.2	0.5	0.3	1.0	13.4	59	10	14	1.0	A/ C–1
Apricot	85.3	1.0	0.3	0.7	1.1	11.6	53	20	25	2.2	A–1.0 2160
Apricot Dried	19.4	1.6	0.7	3.8	2.1	73.4	306	110	70	4.6	A - 5 8 C–2
Bael	61.5	1.8	0.3	1.7	2.9	31.8	137	85	50	0.6	55/8
Banana	70.1	1.2	0.3	0.8	0.4	27.2	116	17	36	0.9	78/7
Cashew Nut	5.9	21.2	46.9	2.4	1.3	22.3	596	50	450	3.6	–
Pine Nut (chilgoza)	4.0	13.9	49.3	2.8	1.0	29.0	615	91	494	3.6	–
Coconut fresh	36.3	4.5	41.6	1.0	3.6	13.0	444	10	240	1.7	0/1

Coconut Tender	90.8	0.9	1.4	0.6	–	6.3	41	10	30	0.9	–/2
Coconut water	93.8	1.4	0.1	0.3	0	4.4	274	24	10	0.1	0/2
Coconut meal	8.7	23.8	2.8	7.0	9.8	47.9	312	112	646	69.6	0/5
Coconut											
Deoited Currants	18.4	2.7	0.5	2.2	1.0	75.2	316	103	110	8.5	21/1
Dates–Dry	15.3	2.5	0.4	2.1	3.9	75.2	317	120	50	7.3	26/3
Figs	88.1	1.3	0.2	0.6	2.2	7.6	37	80	30	1.0	162/5
Grapes	81.2	0.6	0.4	0.9	2.8	13.1	58	20	23	0.5	–/1
Guava	81.7	0.9	0.3	0.7	5.2	11.2	51	10	28	1.4	0/212
Jack Fruit	76.2	0.7	0.3	0.4	1.1	19.8	88	20	41	0.5	175/7
Jambul	83.7	0.7	0.3	0.4	0.9	14.0	62	15	15	1.2	48/18
Lemon	85.0	1.0	0.9	0.3	1.7	11.1	57	70	10	2.3	0/39
Lichi	84.1	1.1	0.2	0.5	0.5	0.5	13.6	61	10	0.7	0/31
Mango	81.0	0.6	0.4	0.4	0.7	16.9	74	14	16	1.3	2743/16
Musk Melon	95.2	0.3	0.2	0.4	0.4	3.5	17	32	14	1.4	169/16
Watermelon	95.8	0.2	0.2	0.3	0.2	3.3	16	11	12	7.9	0/1
Orange	87.6	0.7	0.2	0.3	0.3	10.9	48	26	20	.32	104/30
Orange Juice	97.7	0.2	0.1	0.1	–	1.9	9	5	9	0.7	15/64
Papaya	90.8	0.6	0.1	0.5	0.8	7.2	32	17	13	0.5	666/57
Pea–nut	3.0	25.3	40.1	2.4	3.1	26.1	567	90	350	2.8	37/0
Pine–apple	87.8	0.4	0.1	0.4	0.5	10.8	46	20	9	1.2	18/39
Pistachiq	5.6	19.8	53.5	2.8	2.1	16.2	626	140	430	7.7	144/0
Pomegranate	78.0	1.6	0.1	0.7	5.1	14.5	65	10	70	0.3	0/16
Raisin	20.2	1.8	0.3	2.0	1.1	74.6	308	87	80	7.7	2.4
Strawberry	87.8	0.7	0.2	0.4	1.1	9.8	44	30	30	1.8	11/48
Walnut	4.5	15.6	64.5	1.8	2.6	11.0	687	100	180	4.8	52
Vegetables											
Asparagus	92.0	2.5	0.3	–	–	4.0	23	24	60	0.65	80/20
Beetroot	87.7	1.7	0.1	0.8	0.9	8.8	43	18.3	55	1.0	10/126
Bilter gourd	83.2	2.1	1.0	1.4	1.7	10.6	60	23	38	2.0	126/96
Brinjal	92.7	1.4	0.3	0.3	1.3	4.0	24	18	47	9	74/12
Cabbage	91.9	1.8	0.1	0.6	1.0	4.6	27	39	44	0.8	120/124
Carrot	86.0	0.9	0.2	1.1	1.2	10.6	48	80	530	2.2	1890/3
Cauliflower	90.8	2.6	0.4	1.0	1.2	4.0	30	33	57	1.5	30/56
Celery	93.5	0.8	0.1	0.9	1.2	3.5	18	30	38	4.8	520/6
Cucumber	96.3	0.4	0.1	2.0	4.8	3.7	26	30	110	5.3	110/120
Ginger	80.9	2.3	0.9	1.2	2.4	12.3	67	20	60	2.6	40/0
Goose Foot											

132

(Bathu)	89.6	3.7	0.4	2.6	0.8	2.9	30	150	180	4.2	1740/35
Lady Fingers	89.6	1.9	0.2	0.7	1.2	6.4	35	66	56	1.5	52/13
Mint	84.9	4.8	0.6	1.8	2.00	5.8	48	200	62	15.6	1620/27
Mustard	89.9	4.0	0.6	1.6	0.8	3.2	34	155	26	16.3	2622/33
Onion	84.3	1.8	0.1	0.6	0.6	12.6	59	40	60	1.2	15/2
Peas	72.1	7.2	0.1	0.8	4.0	15.9	93	20	139	1.5	83/9
Potato	74.7	1.6	0.1	0.6	0.4	22.6	97	10	40	.07	50/2
Pumpkin	92.6	1.4	0.1	0.6	0.7	4.6	25	10	30	.07	50/2
Parsley	74.6	5.9	1.0	3.2	1.8	13.5	87	390	175	17.9	1920/281
Radish	94.4	0.7	0.1	0.6	0.8	3.4	17	35	22	0.4	3/15
Radish Leaves	89.1	3.9	0.6	1.6	0.6	4.2	38	310	60	18.0	106/5580
Spinach	92.1	2.0	0.7	1.7	0.6	2.9	26	73	20	10.9	5580/28
Tomato	94.0	0.9	0.2	0.5	0.81	3.0	20	48	20	0.4	351/27
Spices and Condiments											
Asafoetada	16.0	4.0	1.1	7.00	4.1	67.8	297	690	50	22.2	4/0
Cardamom	20.0	10.2	2.2	5.4	20.1	42.1	229	130	160	5.0	–
Chillies–Dry	10.0	15.9	6.2	6.1	30.2	31.6	246	160	370	2.3	345/50
Chillies–green	85.7	2.9	0.6	1.0	6.8	3.0	29	30	80	1.2	195/111
Cinnamon	12.0	12.0	7.8	–	35.0	28.0	229	440	–	17.0	–/–
Cloves	25.2	5.2	8.9	5.2	9.5	46.0	286	740	100	4.9	253/0
Coriander	11.2	14.1	16.1	4.4	32.6	21.6	288	630	393	17.9	942/0
Cumin	11.9	18.7	15.0	5.8	12.0	36.6	356	1080	511	31.0	522/3
Fenugreek Seeds	13.7	26.2	5.8	3.0	7.2	44.1	333	160	370	14.1	96
Garlic	62.0	6.3	0.1	1.0	0.8	29.8	145	30	310	1.3	13
Nutmeg	14.3	7.5	36.4	1.7	11.6	28.5	472	120	240	4.6	0/0
Pepper Dry	13.2	11.5	6.8	4.4	14.9	49.2	304	460	198	16.8	1080/0
Tamarind	20.9	3.1	0.1	2.9	5.6	67.4	283	170	110	10.9	60/3
Turmeric	13.1	6.3	5.1	3.5	2.6	69.4	349	150	282	14.8	30/0
Misc. Foods											
Beaf	8.2	79.2	10.3	1.6	0.5	0.2	410	68	324	18.8	0/0
Biscuit Sweet	5.4	6.4	15.2	1.1	–	71.9	450	–	–	–	–
Bread White	39.0	3.8	0.7	–	0.2	51.9	245	11	–	2.2	–/–
Butter	19.0	–	81.0	2.5	–	–	729	–	–	–	3200
Butter oil	–	–	100	–	–	–	900	–	–	–	2200/0
Cane Sugar											
White	0.4	0.1	0	0.1	0	99.4	398	12	1	–	–
Cheese skimmed											
Milk	77.0	19.5	0.5	–	–	187	90	–		0.4	20/0

Egg	73.7	13.3	13.3	1.0	–	–	173	60	220	2.1	600
Fish Crab	65.3	11.2	9.8	4.6	–	9.1	109	1606	253	–	0/0
Goat Meat	74.2	21.4	3.6	1.1	–	–	118	12	193	–	0/0
Honey	20.6	0.3	0	0.2	–	79.5	319	5	16	0.9	0/4
Jaggery (cane)	3.9	0.4	0.1	0.6	–	95	383	80	40	11.4	168/0
Liver (Sheep)	70.4	19.3	7.5	1.5	–	1.3	150	10	380	6.3	0/20
Mushroom	88.5	3.1	0.8	1.4	0.4	4.3	43	6	110	1.5	0/12
Mutton	71.5	18.5	13.3	1.3	–	–	194	150	150	2.5	0/1400
Milk Powder	3.5	2.58	26.7	6.0	–	38.0	496	950	730	0.6	1400/4
Skimmed milk Powder	401	38.0	0.1	6.8	–	51.0	357	1370	1000	1.4	0/5
Pork	77.4	18.7	4.4	1.0	–	–	114	30	200	2.2	0/2
Poultry Meat	73.0	19.0	7.0	–	–	–	139	15	–	1.5	–/–
Pumpkin Seeds	8.0	24.3	47.2	4.7	0.2	15.6	584	50	830	5.5	38/1
Sugar cane Juice	90.2	0.1	0.2	0.4	–	9.1	39	10	10	1.1	6/1
Water–Melon Seeds	4.3	34.1	52.6	3.7	0.8	4.5	628	100	937	7.4	16
Brewere Yeast–Dried	7.8	35.7	1.8	8.7	–	46.3	344	160	2090	21.5	–
Tempel (Soyabean)	44.0	18.0	7.5	–	–	17.0	195	90	201	2.2	670/0
Toful (Soyabean)	70.0	16.0	9.0	–	–	4.0	140	205	200	12.5	16/0

ENGLISH AND HINDI EQUIVALENTS OF FOOD ITEMS

English	हिन्दी
Acetic acid	सिरका
Acorn	माजूफल
African Cucumber	करेला
Agar-agar	चीनी जड़ी
Alkali	खार
Almonds	बादाम
Alum	फिटकरी
Amaranth	चौलाई
Amonium chloride	नौसादर
Aniseed	सौंफ
Apricot	खुरमानी
Areca-nut	सुपारी
Asafoetida	हींग
Ash gourd	पेठा
Aubergine	बैंगन
Bamboo	बांस
Bamboo shoot	बांस की कोपलें
Banyan	बड़
Barley	जौ
Basil leaves	तुलसी
Bautini	कचनार
Bay leaf	तेजपात
Cluster	गवार फली
Cowgram	लोबिया

English	हिन्दी
French	प्रांस बीन
Hyacinth	सेम
Sword	बड़ी सेम
Beaten rice	चेवड़ा
Beetroot	चुकन्दर
Bengal gram	चना
Betel leaf	पान पत्ता
Betel nut	सुपारी
Bishop's weed	अजवायन
Bitter gourd	करेला
Black salt	काला नमक
Borax	सुहागा
Bran	चोकर
Brinjal	बैंगन
Brown sugar	शक्कर
Bullock's heart	रामफल
Butter	मक्खन
Butter-milk	मट्ठा
Cabbage	बन्द गोभी
Camphor	कपूर
Cape gooseberry	रसभरी
Capsicum	शिमला मिर्च
Carambola	कमरख
Cardamoms (Black)	बड़ी इलायची
Cardamoms (green)	छोटी इलायची
Carom seeds	अजवायन
Carrisa carandas	करोंदा
Carrots	गाजर
Cashwnuts	काजू
Cassia leaves	तेज पत्ता

English	हिन्दी
Castor oil	अरण्डी की तेल
Castor seeds	अरण्डी
Catechu	कत्था
Cauliflower	फूल गोभी
Chilli powder	लाल मिर्च
Cinnamon	दालचीनी
Citric acid	नीम्बू-सत्त
Cloves	लौंग
Cochineal	लाल रंग
Coconut	नारियल
Colocasia	अरबी
Colocasia leaves	अरबी के पत्ते
Condiments	मसाले
Copper sulphate	नीला थोथा
Copra	सूखा नारियल
Coriander powder	हरा धनिया
Corn cob	भुट्टा
Cottage cheese	दही का पनीर
Cotton seeds	बिनौला
Cream	मलाई
Cucumber	खीरा
Cumin seed powder	पिसा ज़ीरी
Cumin seeds	जीरा
Curd	दही
Currants	दाख
Curry leaves	करी पत्ता
Custard apple	शरीफा
Cutch	कत्था
Dates	खजूर
Dill	सोया

English	हिन्दी
Dried apricots	खुमानी
Drumsticks	सहजने की फली
Dry ginger	सोंठ
Egg-plant	बैंगन
Elephant's foot	जिमीकन्द
Essence	सत्त्व
Fennel	सौंफ
Fenugreek leaves	मेथी साग
Fenugreek seeds	मेथी बीज
Figs	अंजीर
Flea seeds	ईसबगोल
Garlic	लहुसन
Gingelly Seasamum oil	तिल का तेल
Ginger (fresh)	अदरक
Ginder (dry)	सोंठ
Gooseberry	रसभरी
Gourd (ash)	पेठा
Gourd (bitter)	करेला
Gourd (pointed)	परवल
Gourd (red)	लाल कद्दू
Gourd (sponge)	घिया/तोराई
Gourd (wax)	पेठा
Gram	चना
Gram flour	बेसन
Grapes	अंगूर/दाख
Gravy	शोरबा
Green Chillies	हरी मिर्च
Greens	साग
Groundnuts	मूंगफली
Gruel	मांड

English	हिन्दी
Hazelnut (Chinese)	लीची
Henna	मेहंदी
Hog-plum	आंवला
Jackfruit	कटहल
Jaggery	गुड़
Jujube	बेर
Khol rabi / khol khol	गांठ गोबी

❑❑❑

A Mantra to Develop Brain

Biswaroop Roy Chowdhury, an authority in brain and learning techniques and National Memory Record holder, combines ancient wisdom and latest scientific Key Techiniques of Memory (KTM) as a way to memory development. In his book **'Dynamic Memory Methods'**, the young Memory Consultant has given tips regarding the use of scientific memory techniques for memorising faster and retaining it longer. Based on mnemonics (artificial aids to learning) and laws of controlled association, the simple mental exrcises mentioned in the book enhance the reader's observation and concentration in an amazing way. The regular practice of various techniques mentioned inculcates the babit of using creative (Right) part of brain and thus the brain's capacity is optimized owing to balanced use of both logical (Left) and creative part of the brain. The book teaches 100 memory codes of memory language which help the readers in developing mental catalogue so that they can make their recalling and remembering effective.

The book is useful for all, a business person or a student, young or old; as familiarity with the memory language also helps in remembering telephone numbers, vocabulary, names and faces, speeches and anecdotes more efficiently.

Some of the interesting features of the book include:

- Making learning a fun
- Advanced Mnemonic System
- Curing absent-mindedness
- Increase in intellect and positive mental attitude

- How to study smarter and not harder
- Preparing for competitive exams
- Remembering long answers of history
- Memorising geographical maps & biological diagrams

ALSO AVAILABLE IN HINDI & BENGALI

Order books by V.P.P. Postage Rs. 20/- per book extra. Postage free on order of three or more books.

⊚ FUSION BOOKS

X-30, Okhla Industrial Area, Phase-II, New Delhi-110 020
Phone : 011-51611861, Fax : 011-51611866
E-mail : manish@diamondpublication.com, Website : www.fusionbooks.com

DIAMOND POCKET BOOKS PRESENTS

BOOKS FOR ALL

K. R. Wadhwaney
Indian Cricket Controversies 195.00
Mainak Dhar
Flash Point 195.00
Jagdish Sharma
Body Language 195.00
L.R. Chowdhary
Kundalini Mantra Yoga 95.00
Shiv Sharma
Soul of Sikhism 125.00
Soul of Jainism 125.00
Biswaroop Roy Chowdhury
Memorising Dictionary Made Easy 150.00
Dr. Bimal Chajjer
Zero Oil Cook Book *(300 pages)* 150.00
B. K. Chaturvedi
Srimad Bhagwat Puran 95.00
Agni Purana 75.00
PATANJALI YOGA SUTRA
Yoga - The Alpha and The Omega-I
(The Birth of Being) 150.00
Yoga - The Alpha and The Omega-II
(The Ever Present Flower) 150.00
Yoga - The Alpha and The Omega-III
(Moving to the Centre) 150.00
VEDANTA
Vedanta : The Ultimate Truth ... 50.00
Vedanta : The First Star in the
Evening 50.00
M. Subramaniam
Unveiling the Secrets of Reiki . 195.00
Brilliant Light 195.00
(Reiki Grand Master Manual)
Dr. Shiv Kumar
Causes and Cure of Stress 95.00
Acharya Bhagwan Dev
Yoga for Better Health 95.00

Dr. Pushpa Khurana
Be Young and Healthy for 100 Years 60.00
Shashi Kant Oak
Naadi Predction 95.00
Dr. Bhojraj Dwivedi
Hindu Traditions and Beliefs : A Scientific
Validity *(Questions & Answers)* 150.00 •
Feng Shui : Chinese Vaastu Shastra 195.00
Thumb! The Mirror of Fate 150.00
Cheiro
Cheiro's Language of the
Hand *(Palmistry)* 95.00
Dr. B.R. Kishore
India - A Travel Guide 395.00
Lokesh Thani & Rajshekhar Mishra
Sensational Sachin 60.00
Virendar Kumar
Kargil : The Untold Story *(Rape of
the Mountains; With Pictures)* ... 95.00
B. Umamashwara Rao
The Spiritual Philosophy of
Shri Shirdi Sai Baba 150.00
Thus Spake Sri Shirdi Sai Baba . 40.00
HUMOUR SERIES
Laughing Jokes 60.00
Naughty Jokes 60.00
Society Jokes 60.00
Children Jokes 60.00
Delighting Jokes 60.00
Thrilling Jokes 60.00
Hilarious Jokes 60.00
Spicy Jokes 60.00
Crispy Jokes 60.00
T.V. Queen Tabassum
Tabassum's Jokes 35.00
Raj Gopal Katju
Katju's Follies 60.00
Katju's Whims 60.00

**Order books by V.P.P. Postage Rs. 20/- per book extra.
Postage free on order of three or more books. Send Rs. 20/--in advance.**

DIAMOND POCKET BOOKS (P) LTD.
X-30, Okhla Industrial Area, Phase-II, New Delhi-110020.
Phones : 51611861-65, Fax : (0091) -011- 51611866, 26386124

DIAMOND POCKET BOOKS PRESENTS

BOOKS FOR ALL

K. R. Wadhwaney
Indian Cricket Controversies 195.00
Mainak Dhar
Flash Point 195.00
Jagdish Sharma
Body Language 195.00
L.R. Chowdhary
Kundalini Mantra Yoga 95.00
Shiv Sharma
Soul of Sikhism 125.00
Soul of Jainism 125.00
Biswaroop Roy Chowdhury
Memorising Dictionary Made Easy 150.00
Dr. Bimal Chajjer
Zero Oil Cook Book *(300 pages)* 150.00
B. K. Chaturvedi
Srimad Bhagwat Puran 95.00
Agni Purana 75.00
PATANJALI YOGA SUTRA
Yoga - The Alpha and The Omega-I
(The Birth of Being) 150.00
Yoga - The Alpha and The Omega-II
(The Ever Present Flower) 150.00
Yoga - The Alpha and The Omega-III
(Moving to the Centre) 150.00
VEDANTA
Vedanta : The Ultimate Truth ... 40.00
Vedanta : The First Star in the
Evening 40.00
M. Subramaniam
Unveiling the Secrets of Reiki . 195.00
Brilliant Light 195.00
(Reiki Grand Master Manual)
Dr. Shiv Kumar
Causes and Cure of Stress 95.00
Acharya Bhagwan Dev
Yoga for Better Health 95.00

Dr. Pushpa Khurana
Be Young and Healthy for 100 Years 60.00
Shashi Kant Oak
Naadi Predction 95.00
Dr. Bhojraj Dwivedi
Hindu Traditions and Beliefs : A Scientific
Validity *(Questions & Answers)* 150.00
Feng Shui : Chinese Vaastu Shastra 195.00
Thumb! The Mirror of Fate 150.00
Cheiro
Cheiro's Language of the
Hand *(Palmistry)* 95.00
Dr. B.R. Kishore
India - A Travel Guide 395.00
Lokesh Thani & Rajshekhar Mishra
Sensational Sachin 60.00
Virendar Kumar
Kargil : The Untold Story *(Rape of
the Mountains; With Pictures)* ... 95.00
B.Umamashwara Rao
The Spiritual Philosophy of
Shri Shirdi Sai Baba 150.00
Thus Spake Sri Shirdi Sai Baba . 40.00
HUMOUR SERIES
Laughing Jokes 60.00
Naughty Jokes 60.00
Society Jokes 60.00
Children Jokes 60.00
Delighting Jokes 60.00
Thrilling Jokes 60.00
Hilarious Jokes 60.00
Spicy Jokes 60.00
Crispy Jokes 60.00
T. V. Queen Tabassum
Tabassum's Jokes 35.00
Raj Gopal Katju
Katju's Follies 60.00
Katju's Whims 60.00

Order books by V.P.P. Postage Rs. 20/- per book extra.
Postage free on order of three or more books. Send Rs. 20/- in advance.

DIAMOND POCKET BOOKS (P) LTD.
X-30, Okhla Industrial Area, Phase-II, New Delhi-110020.
Phones : 51611861-65, Fax : (0091) -011- 51611866, 26386124

Cultural Diversity of India

India-A Travel Guide

India, the seventh largest country in the world is so fantastic in its variety, colors, dresses, deities, climates and languages that it becomes an amazingly inexhaustible experience.

India with its 330 million Hindu gods and goddesses, is a land of inimitable records. It has been a meeting point of various cultures, civilizations and religions for more than five millennia.

395/-

Tourist Centres of India

No country in the world can boast of such varied climates, dissimilar country sides and rich heritage. But when the tourists land in our country they get rather confused by the lack of information and guidance. It is to fill this lacunae that this book is devised in five broad sections or zones for the convenience of the visitors. The tourist spots of the entire country have been divided into Delhi, Kolkata, Mumbai, Chennai and Bangalore zones. The idea is that a tourist reaching Delhi may visit all the spots, easily accessible from Delhi and then may go to the other zones.

60/-

Pilgrimage Centres of India

95/-

The vast number of Hindu gods and goddesses may confound a stranger, but in reality they represent the different aspects of the One and the same Supreme Being. He is the One and Omnipresent. The trinity of Brahma, Vishnu and Shiva represents the three-creative, preservative and destructive aspects of the one Supreme Bing.

परिक्रमा उत्तराखंड

150/-

भारत भूमि को देवताओं की भूमि कहा जाता है। आध्यात्मिकता के क्षेत्र में भी भारत विश्व गुरु कहलाता है। इसके उत्तराखंड क्षेत्र का अपने आपमें विशेष महत्त्व हैं। उत्तराखंड मुख्य रूप से पर्वतीय क्षेत्र है जिसमे कुमाऊं एवं गढ़वाल पहाड़ियां हैं। यहां की प्राकृतिक छटा तथा अध्यात्मिकता सैलानियों को बरबस अपनी ओर खींचती है। यहां के प्राकृतिक सौंदर्य के बीच अध्यात्मिक केन्द्र तथा मंदिरों ने उत्तराखंड की पर्यटन के क्षेत्र में विशेष पहचान बनाई है।

Order Books by V.P.P.. Postage Rs. 20/- per book. Postage free on order of 3 or more books, ask for a free catalogue

DIAMOND BOOKS

X-30, Okhla Industrial Area, Phase-II, New Delhi - 110020,
Tel: (011) 51611861-865, 26386289, Fax: 011-51611866,
Email-nverma@nde.vsnl.net.in, Website : www.diamondpocketbooks.com

DIAMOND BOOKS PRESENTS

David Servan Schreiber 'Gurier'
- [ ] The Instinct to Heal 195.00
  (Curing stress, anxiety and depression
  without drugs and without talk therapy)

Swati Lodha
- [ ] Why Women Are What
  They Are 195.00

Osho
- [ ] Yoga - The Alchemy of Yoga .150.00

Dr. Bimal Chhajer
- [ ] 201 Diet Tips for
  Heart Patients 150.00

Joginder Singh
- [ ] Jokes of Joginder singh (I, II) ... 95.00

Pandit Atre
- [ ] Soul @ Universe.Com 75.00

M.G. Devasahayam
- [ ] India's IInd Freedom
  an Untold Saga 195.00

Vandana Verma
- [ ] Lovely Names for Male &
  Female childs 95.00

BOOKS ON HINDU MYTHOLOGY

Prafull Goradia
- [ ] The Saffron Book 150.00
- [ ] Anti Hindus 150.00
- [ ] Muslim League's
  Unfinished Agenda 150.00
- [ ] Hindu Masjids 195.00

Dr. Brij Raj Kishore
- [ ] Essence of Vedas 195.00

S. N. Mathur
- [ ] The Diamond Books of Hindu Gods
  and Goddesses (4 Colour) 295.00

B.K. Chaturvedi
- [ ] Shiva Purana 95.00
- [ ] Vishnu Purana 95.00
- [ ] Markandeya Purana 75.00
- [ ] Bhsvishya Purana 75.00
- [ ] Narad Purana 75.00
- [ ] Kalki Purana 75.00
- [ ] Linga Purana 75.00

LITERATURE

Rabindranath Tagore
- [ ] Boat Accident (Translation
  of नौका डूबी) 95.00
- [ ] Inside Outside (Translation
  of घरे बाइरे) 95.00

Iqbal Ramoowalia
- [ ] The Death Of A Passport 150.00

Ed. Rajendra Awasthy
- [ ] Selected Gujrati Short Stories 95.00
- [ ] Selected Hindi Short Stories 125.00
- [ ] Selected Tamil Short Stories 95.00
- [ ] Selected Malayalam Short
  Stories 95.00
- [ ] Selected Punjabi Short Stories ... 95.00

K. S. Duggal
- [ ] Birth of a Song 95.00

GREAT PERSONALITIES
(BIOGRAPHY)

Anuradha Ray
- [ ] The Making of Mahatma
  (A Biography) 95.00

Prof. Gurpreet Singh
- [ ] Ten Masters (Sikh Gurus) 60.00
- [ ] The Soul of Sikhism 95.00

B.K. Chaturvedi
- [ ] Messiah of Poor Mother Teresa 60.00
- [ ] Chanakya 95.00
- [ ] Goddess Durga 95.00

S.P. Bansal
- [ ] Lord Rama 95.00
- [ ] Gajanan 75.00

Dr. Brij Raj Kishore
- [ ] Ram Krishna Paramhans 95.00

Purnima Majumdaar
- [ ] Yogiraj Arvind 75.00
- [ ] Neel Kanth (Lord Shiva) 95.00

Dr. Bhwan Singh Rana
- [ ] Swami Vivekanand 120.00
- [ ] Chhatrapati Shivaji 95.00
- [ ] Bhagat Singh 95.00

Mahesh Sharma
- [ ] Dr. A.P.J. Abdul Kalam 95.00
- [ ] Sonia Gandhi 95.00
- [ ] Atal Bihari Vajpayee 95.00
- [ ] Lal Krishna Advani 95.00

Books can be requisitioned by V.P.P. Postage charges will be Rs. 20/- per book. For orders of three books the postage will be free.

DIAMOND POCKET BOOKS

X-30, Okhla Industrial Area, Phase-II, New Delhi-110020, Phone : 011-51611861, Fax : 011-51611866
E-mail : sales@diamondpublication.com, Website : www.fusionbooks.com